HUMAN BEHAVIOR
AND
BRAIN FUNCTION

Edited by

HARVEY J. WIDROE, M.D.

Medical Director
Walnut Creek Psychiatric Hospital
Walnut Creek, California

CHARLES C THOMAS • PUBLISHER
Springfield • Illinois • U.S.A.

Published and Distributed Throughout the World by
CHARLES C THOMAS • PUBLISHER
Bannerstone House
301-327 East Lawrence Avenue, Springfield, Illinois, U.S.A.

© *1975, by* CHARLES C THOMAS • PUBLISHER

ISBN 0-398-03271-8

Library of Congress Catalog Card Number: 74-18324

Printed in the United States of America
R-1

Library of Congress Cataloging in Publication Data
Main entry under title:

Human behavior and brain function.

   Proceedings of a symposium held May 12, 1973, at
Walnut Creek Hospital, Walnut Creek, Calif.
   1. Psychology, Physiological — Congresses.
2. Brain — Congresses.   I. Widroe, Harvey J., ed.
[DNLM: 1. Behavior — Congresses. 2. Brain
Physiology
— Congresses.   WL300 H9176 1973]
QP360.H85   612'.82   74-18324
ISBN 0-398-03271-8

CONTRIBUTORS

GEORGE BACH-Y-RITA, M.D.: Assistant Clinical Professor of Psychiatry, University of California, San Francisco, California.

ENOCH CALLAWAY, M.D.: Chief of Research, Langley-Porter Neuropsychiatric Institute; Professor of Psychiatry in Residence, University of California Medical Center, San Francisco, California.

DAVID GALIN, M.D.: Research Specialist, Langley-Porter Neuropsychiatric Institute; Member of the Institute for the Study of Human Consciousness.

HARDIN JONES, Ph.D.: Professor of Medical Physics and Physiology, University of California, Berkeley, California; Assistant Director of Donner Laboratory, University of California, Berkeley, California.

GERHARDT VON BONIN, M.D.: Professor Emeritus, University of Illinois, Department of Anatomy; Consultant in Neuroanatomy, Mt. Zion Medical Center, San Francisco, California.

EUGENE VOLTOLINA, M.D.: Director of Neuropsychiatric Research, Oakland Naval Hospital, Oakland, California.

HARVEY J. WIDROE, M.D.: Medical Director, Walnut Creek Psychiatric Hospital, Walnut Creek, California.

VINCENT ZARCONE, M.D.: Assistant Professor, Department of Psychiatry, Stanford Medical Center, Stanford, California.

FOREWORD

Every science goes through certain developmental phases. Early in the development of a particular science its practitioners have little substantive knowledge to give them comfort, and out of a sense of insecurity they cling tenaciously to what few fragments of knowledge they actually have. They arrange these fragments in a barely organized form and call it "truth," which is to be defended from other versions of "truth" and most certainly from the inroads of factual observation. Thus, each science in its early stages of development finds its adherents and its investigators huddled in cults — each proclaiming its own virtues and denouncing the claims of all others as fallacious and even blasphemous. In mathematics the followers of Pythagoras energetically disputed with the followers of Heraclitus. In physics those who proclaimed the particle theory of energy transmission as "truth" quarreled vigorously with those who supported the wave theory concept.

Only recently has psychiatry made any substantive move out of the cultism phase of development. Even now, while cultism in psychiatry is dying, it is putting up a most vigorous resistance. As recently as fifteen years ago psychiatric practitioners were divided into two major camps: organicists versus psychoanalysts. Organicists believed that all mental illnesses had organic etiologies, possibly genetically determined, and that organic modes of treatment were always indicated. In contrast, the analysts believed environmentally determined intrapsychic conflict to be fundamental to mental illness, and that psychological modalities of treatment were always indicated. Organicists and analysts rarely spoke to one another. The organicists were viewed by the analysts as insensitive sadists who kept patients in asylums, while the analysts were viewed by the organicists as charlatans and fools who never dealt with patients

vii

suffering from serious mental illness. At that time if one dared to declare oneself to be an eclectic, it was tantamount to a confession of knowing nothing about anything at all.

But in the last fifteen years the development of psychopharmacological agents more than any other factor has enabled psychiatry to develop a respectable eclecticism, the pronouncements of which stand less on declarations of faith in dogma and more on the dialectical progression of organization and explication of fact. In that eclecticism we are less concerned with naive questions which have been the product of the schisms of the past, such as, "Is the etiology of this psychopathological behavior functional or organic?", or, "Is mental illness genetically determined or is it environmentally determined?"

Instead, our appreciation of multiple parameters for describing a behavioral event has posed questions which are far more complex, but at the same time closer approximations to the clinical issues before us. For example, we now ask, "Do genes affect behavior by influencing the production of specific enzymes in the brain which make neurons more capable of growth as a product of incoming environmental stimuli?" Or, "Do amphetamines increase the attention span of hyperkinetic children by selectively increasing the transmission of norepinephrine?" Or, "Is assaultive and homicidal behavior in man mediated through the amygdaloid nucleus of the nondominant hemisphere?" Or, "Can character pathology be understood as maladaptive patterns of behavior (nonresponsive to environmental stimuli) which are stored as polypeptide configurations in the cortex?"

These breathtaking questions challenge us to comprehend terms and concepts which only a few years ago could not meaningfully be related in the same statement. Perhaps these questions will turn out to be fruitless science fiction. Yet these are the types of questions our investigators force us to examine today. It is my sincere hope that this collection of papers will stimulate the reader to clearer observations and formulations which ultimately will bear clinically applicable fruit.

H.J.W.

CONTENTS

HUMAN BEHAVIOR
AND
BRAIN FUNCTION

Chapter 1

HEMISPHERIC SPECIALIZATION AND THE DUALITY OF CONSCIOUSNESS

DAVID GALIN AND ROBERT E. ORNSTEIN

A VARIETY of evidence from clinical and neurosurgical sources indicates that the two hemispheres of the human brain are specialized for different cognitive functions. This evidence has been confirmed in studies of normal subjects. The left hemisphere is predominantly involved in verbal and other analytic functions, the right in spatial and other holistic processing.

The two hemispheres have been surgically separated for the treatment of certain cases of epilepsy; after the operation it has been found that each hemisphere is conscious and can carry out complex cognitive processes of the type for which it is specialized. In short, there appear to be two separate, conscious minds in one head. The study of how these two half-brains cooperate or interfere with each other in normal, intact people has just begun. We believe that this work has important implications for psychiatric theory and practice, and education, as well as for clinical neurology.

In our laboratory at Langley Porter we have been studying this lateralization of function with EEG techniques. With the method which we have developed we can distinguish between these two cognitive modes as they occur in normal subjects, using simple scalp recordings.

We will review some of the experiments and clinical observations on this duality in human nature and mention some of the opportunities for future research that seem to us most promising.

SPECIALIZATION OF THE TWO HEMISPHERES — "SPLIT-BRAIN" STUDIES

The asymmetrical localization of cognitive function has long been established. Language was ascribed to the left hemisphere by Dax in 1836 (1). Since then clinical work with brain-damaged patients has continued to differentiate the cognitive functions of the hemispheres (2, 3, 4, 5). For example, right temporal lobectomy produces a severe impairment on visual and tactile mazes. In contrast, left temporal lobectomy of equal extent produces little deficit on these tasks but impairs verbal memory (3, 5). In general, clinical work has found that verbal and arithmetical functions (analytic, linear) depend on the left hemisphere, while spatial relationships (holistic, gestalt) are the special province of the right hemisphere. Sperry, Gazzaniga, and Bogen (6) and their associates (7, 8) have had a unique opportunity to study the specialization of the two halves of the brain isolated from each other. They worked with patients who had undergone surgical section of the corpus callosum for the treatment of epilepsy. These "split brain" patients were tested with a special apparatus to insure that the task was presented to only one hemisphere at a time. Sperry, Gazzaniga, and Bogen have been able to establish that each hemisphere can function independently and is independently conscious. Learning and memory are found to continue separately in each hemisphere. The right hand literally does not know what the left hand is doing. Both halves independently sense, perceive, and conceptualize. Unilateral associations between tactual, visual, and auditory sensations remain. In these patients, the left hemisphere is capable of speech, writing, and mathematical calculation and is severely limited in problems involving spatial relations. The right hemisphere has use of only a few words and can perform simple addition only up to ten, but can perform tasks involving spatial relationships and musical patterns.

It is important to emphasize that what most characterizes the hemispheres is not that they are specialized to work with different types of material (the left with words and the right with spatial forms); rather each hemisphere is specialized for a different cognitive style: the left for an analytic, logical mode for which words are an excellent tool, and the right for a holistic, gestalt mode, which happens to be particularly suitable for spatial relations and music. The difference in cognitive style is explicitly described in a recent paper by Levy, Trevarthen, and Sperry (9):

> Recent commissurotomy studies have shown that the two
> disconnected hemispheres, working on the same task, may
> process the same sensory information in distinctly different
> ways, and that the two modes of mental operation involving
> spatial synthesis for the right and temporal analysis for the left,
> show indications of mutual antagonism (7). The propensity of
> the language hemisphere to note analytical details in a way that
> facilitates their description in language seems to interfere with
> the perception of an over-all Gestalt, leaving the left
> hemisphere "unable to see the wood for the trees." This
> interference effect suggested a rationale for the evolution of
> lateral specialization . . . (Also see Nebes (10) and Semmes (11).)

Sperry and his collaborators have found that "in general, the
postoperative behavior of (the commissurotomy patients) has
been dominated by the major (left) hemisphere ..." except in
tasks for which the right hemisphere is particularly specialized
(9).

To understand the method of testing and interviewing each
half of the brain separately, two points of functional anatomy
must be kept in mind. The first is that since language functions
(speech, writing) are mediated predominantly by the left
hemisphere in most people, the disconnected right hemisphere
cannot express itself verbally. The second point is that the neural
pathways carrying information from one side of the body and one
half of the visual field cross over and connect only with the
opposite side of the brain. This means that sensations in the right
hand and images in the right visual space will be projected almost
entirely to the *left* hemisphere. Similarly, the major motor output
is crossed, and the left hemisphere mainly controls the
movements of the right hand. Therefore, patients with the corpus
callosum sectioned can describe or answer questions about
objects placed in their right hands or pictures flashed to the right
visual field with a tachistoscope, but can give no correct verbal
response when the information is presented to the left hand or the
left visual field (they will, in fact, often confabulate). The mute
right hemisphere can, however, indicate its experience with the
left hand, for example, by selecting the proper object from an array.

Dissociation of Experience

The dissociation between the experiences of the two disconnected hemispheres is sometimes very dramatic. A film made by Sperry and his colleagues shows two illustrative incidents.

The film shows a young female patient being tested with a tachistoscope as described above. In the series of neutral geometrical figures being presented at random to the right and left fields, a nude pin-up was included and flashed to the right (nonverbal) hemisphere. The girl blushed and giggled. Sperry asked "What did you see?" She answered "Nothing, just a flash of light," and giggled again, covering her mouth with her hand. "Why are you laughing then?" asks Sperry, and she laughs again and says, "Oh, Dr. Sperry, you have some machine!" The episode is very dramatic, and if one did not know her neurosurgical history one might have seen this as a clear example of perceptual defense: one might infer that she was repressing the perception of the conflictful sexual material — even her final response (a socially acceptable nonsequitur) was convincing. (Also see Sperry (12), especially p. 732.)

In another section of the film a different patient is performing a block design task; he is trying to match a colored geometric design with a set of painted blocks. The film shows the left hand (right hemisphere) quickly carrying out the task. Then the experimenter disarranges the blocks and the right hand (left hemisphere) is given the task; slowly and with great apparent indecision it arranges the pieces. In trying to match a corner of the design the right hand corrects one of the blocks, and then shifts it again, apparently not realizing it was correct: the viewer sees the left hand dart out, grab the block to restore it to the correct position — and then the arm of the experimenter reaches over and pulls the intruding left hand off-camera.

Psychiatric Implications

There is a compelling formal similarity between these dissociation phenomena seen in the commissurotomy patients and the phenomena of repression; according to Freud's early "topographical" model of the mind, repressed mental contents functioned in a separate realm which was inaccessible to conscious recall or verbal interrogation, functioned according to its own rules, developed and pursued its own goals, affected the viscera, and insinuated itself in the stream of ongoing consciously directed behavior.

This parallel suggests that we examine the hypothesis that in normal, intact people mental events in the right hemisphere can become disconnected functionally from the left hemisphere (by inhibition of neuronal transmission across the corpus callosum and other cerebral commissures) and can continue a life of their own. This hypothesis suggests a neurophysiological mechanism for at least some cases of repression and an anatomical locus for the unconscious mental contents.

What are the circumstances under which such a dissociation could take place? There are several ways in which the two hemispheres of an ordinary person could begin to function as if they had been surgically disconnected and cease exchanging information. The first way is by active inhibition of information transfer because of conflict. Imagine the effect on a child when his mother presents one message verbally, but quite another with her facial expression and body language; "I am doing it because I love you, dear," says the words, but "I hate you and will destroy you" says the face. Each hemisphere is exposed to the same sensory input, but because of its relative specializations, each emphasizes only one of the messages. The left will attend to the verbal cues because it cannot extract information from the facial gestalt efficiently; the right will attend preferentially to the nonverbal cues because it cannot easily understand the words (9). Effectively, a different input has been delivered to each hemisphere, just as in the laboratory experiments in which a tachistoscope is used to present different pictures to the left and right visual fields. We offer the following conjecture: In this situation the two hemispheres might decide on opposite courses of action; the left to approach, and the right to flee. Because of the high stakes involved, each hemisphere might be able to maintain its consciousness and resist the inhibitory influence of the other side.

The left hemisphere seems to win control of the output channels most of the time (12), but if the left is not able to "turn off" the right completely it may settle for disconnecting the transfer of the conflicting information from the other side. The connections between hemispheres are relatively weak compared to the connections within hemispheres (8), and it seems likely that each hemisphere treats the weak contralateral input in the same way in which people in general treat the odd, discrepant observation which does not fit with the mass of their beliefs; first we ignore it, and then if it is insistent, we actively avoid it (13).

The mental process in the right hemisphere, cut off in this way from the left hemisphere consciousness which is directly overt behavior, may nevertheless continue a life of its own. The memory of the situation, the emotional concomitants, and the frustrated plan of action all may persist, affecting subsequent perception and forming the basis for expectations and evaluations of future input.

Active inhibition arising from conflicting goals is not the only way to account for a lack of communication between the two hemispheres and the consequent divergence of consciousness. In the simplest case, because of their special modes of organization and special areas of competence, the knowledge which one hemisphere possesses may not translate well into the language of the other. For example, the experience of attending a symphony concert is not readily expressed in words, and the concept "Democracy requires informed participation" is hard to convey in images. What may be transmitted in such cases may be the conclusion as to action and not the details on which the evaluation was based. It is possible to convey some of the richness of the holistic consciousness in words, but it requires a great artist.

NEO-PHRENOLOGY

It is not clear to what extent specific cognitive performances can be said to depend on specific areas of the cerebrum, beyond the gross distinction between left and right hemispheres. Without going too far in the direction of assigning "centers" to each mental quality in the manner of the phrenologists, there seems to be some evidence for within-hemisphere localization. For example, Milner (14) has correlated disorders in specific kinds of language processing with lesions in specific areas of the left hemisphere: verbal memory deficits with anterior temporal lesions, speech deficits with posterior temporal lesions, fluency deficits with frontal lesions, and reading deficits with lesions in the region of the parieto-occipital junction.

The difficulties inherent in "localizing" complex functions are exemplified in the conflicting literature on the lateralization of arithmetic calculation. Luria finds "primary acalculia" or primary arithmetical disturbances with lesions of the left infero-parietal lobe (4), but Kinsbourne (15) finds no systematic lateralization for arithmetic.

The problem is complex, according to Critchley (16) because calculation may entail more than one type of mentation, and different people seem to employ different methods. Lesions in different areas would be expected to produce dyscalculia insofar as a person depends on the use of specific visual symbols or notation or on rote memory (e.g. multiplication tables) or on an ideokinetic factor based on concrete manipulation, such as counting on fingers. The horizontal and vertical arrangement of numbers to represent units — tens, hundreds, etc. — depends on spatial and constructional factors. Vivid imagery for numerical forms and sequences may be important to some people (17). Critchley concludes, "Nonetheless, there are certain 'vulnerable' regions of the brain, wherein a lesion is more apt to be followed by a severe dyscalculia bearing certain clinical hallmarks. Thus, disease of the dominant left hemisphere is more often followed by severe disorders of calculation (16)."

EVIDENCE FOR LATERAL SPECIALIZATION
IN NORMAL PEOPLE

Some caution should be exercised in making the inference of lateral specialization of cognitive function in normal people from lesion studies alone. One might consider whether the "split" functions are due in some part to the radical surgery or to the other disturbances in these patients. The study of neurological disorders or surgical preparations cast light on normal functioning, but the most important and most practical question is whether the normal brain, engaged in everyday activities, is organized around lateralization of cognitive function.

Recent research with normal subjects provides support for the inference that the intact brain does in fact make use of lateral specialization. With normal subjects, Filbey and Gazzaniga have measured the time required for information presented to one hemisphere to be acted upon by the other. A verbal reaction to information presented to the nonverbal right hemisphere took longer than a nonverbal response (18). McKeever found faster tachistoscopic word recognition for words projected to the left hemisphere than to the right (19). In dichotic listening tasks, normal subjects have better recall for verbal material presented to the right than to the left ear and better recall for melodies presented to the left (20).

Other laboratories have used electrophysiological techniques such as evoked potentials and DC potentials. Buchsbaum recorded average visual evoked potentials from the left and right occipital areas in response to words and geometric stimuli (21). The responses to these two classes of stimuli were the same in the right hemisphere, but different in the left hemisphere. Wood, et al. (22) found similar results with auditory stimuli; subjects listened to verbal stimuli under two conditions to process them for speech cues (stop consonants) and for nonspeech cues (pitch). The evoked responses were the same in the right hemisphere, but different in the left hemisphere.

Morrell and Salamy (23) reported that evoked potentials to speech sounds were larger in the left hemisphere leads than in the right, and Vella, et al. (24) reported that responses to complex visual forms were larger in the right. McAdam and Whitaker recorded DC potentials over the left and right frontotemporal areas. Just before subjects spoke, a negative shift appeared, more pronounced on the left than on the right. No shift was seen preceding nonverbal vocal tract activities (voluntary coughing, spitting) (25).

In the past three years we have applied EEG methods to the

study of this lateral specialization in normal people. By studying EEG asymmetry we have been able to distinguish the two cognitive modes as they occur in normal subjects using simple scalp recording (26). In brief, we examined the EEGs of subjects performing verbal and spatial tasks to determine whether there were differences in activity between the appropriate and inappropriate hemispheres. We recorded from the temporal and parietal areas since clinico-anatomical evidence indicates that these areas should be differently engaged in these tasks. We found that during verbal tasks the integrated whole-band power in the left hemisphere is less than that in the right, and during spatial tasks the integrated power in the right hemisphere is less than in the left. Most of the task-dependent asymmetry appeared to be in the alpha band. Our method of analyzing the ratios of right to left EEG power was adopted by McKee, Humphrey, and McAdam (27) in a study contrasting musical and verbal processing. They confirm our general finding that the ratio is higher in the verbal tasks compared to the nonverbal task.

Table 1-I summarizes some of the results from two of our experiments. The average alpha ratios (right/left) were computed for temporal, parietal, and central recordings during verbal and spatial tasks intended to engage primarily the left or the right hemisphere. Spatial tasks were intended to engage primarily the right hemisphere. Spatial tasks included building geometric designs from memory with blocks, mirror drawing and a mental Form Board task. Verbal tasks included composing a letter mentally and in writing and memorizing and writing the main facts from a text passage. The task pairs which were selected differ in their requirement for motor output and for memory. The attention-to-breathing task was included as a "neutral" noncognitive condition. (For further details of the methods and results of Experiment 1, see Galin and Ornstein (26) and Doyle, Ornstein, and Galin (28).)

Figure 1-1 shows a sample from the EEG from one subject during the Blocks and Written Letter tasks. Figure 1-2 shows the results of frequency spectrum analysis of the EEG from which Figure 1-1 was taken.

The second experiment confirms the main effect found in the

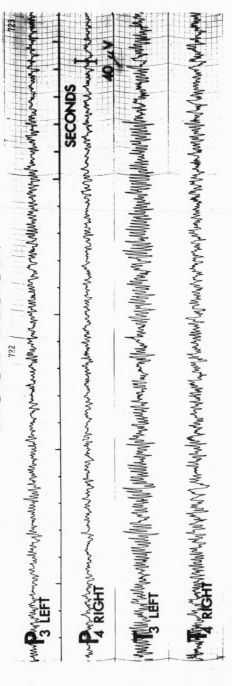

Figure 1-1. Change in EEG asymmetry during the Blocks (A) and Written Letter (B) Tasks: P_3 = left parietal, P_4 = right parietal, T_3 = left temporal, T_4 = right temporal. The ratio of power in homologous leads T_4/T_3 and P_4/P_3 is greater on the spatial task than on the verbal task. (Reprinted with permission from D. Galin and R. Ornstein, "Lateral Specialization of Cognitive Mode: An EEG Study," *Psychophysiology*, vol. 9 [1972], pp. 412-418.)

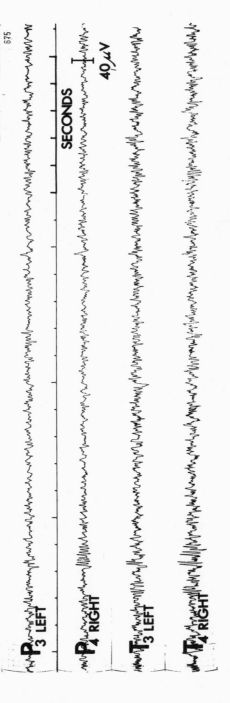

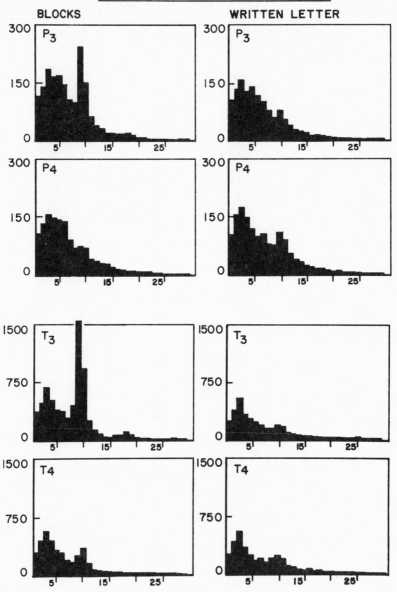

Figure 1-2. Sample Fourier power spectra for Blocks and Written Letter tasks. For each lead, EEG power is plotted versus frequency in 1 Hz intervals from 1 to 29 Hz; the last point on each plot is an average for frequencies 30 to 64 Hz. The ordinate is scaled in arbitrary units in which a 10 Hz sine wave of eighty microvolts p-p corresponds to 80,000 units. The ratio of alpha-band power from homologous leads T_4/T_3 and P_4/P_3 is greater on the Blocks task than on the Written Letter task. These spectra correspond to the sample EEG tracings shown in Figure 1-1. (Reprinted with permission from J. C. Doyle, R. Ornstein and D. Galin, "Lateral Specialization of Cognitive Mode: II. EEG Frequency Analysis," *Psychophysiology* [1973], in press).

TABLE 1-I

INTER- AND INTRA-HEMISPHERIC SPECIALIZATION FOR COGNITIVE MODE: DIFFERENCES BETWEEN ELECTRODE LOCATIONS - ALPHA RATIOS*

Experiment I

		Motor tasks			*Mental tasks*		"*Noncognitive*"
N = 10	Blocks	Written letter	p	Form Board	Mental Letter	p	Attention to-Breath
P4/P3	0.97	1.09	.01	0.81	0.98	ns	0.94
T4/T3	0.68	1.06	.01	0.79	1.06	.05	0.87

Experiment II

		Memory tasks			*Nonmemory tasks*		"*Noncognitive*"
N = 35	Blocks	Write from Memory	p	Mirror Drawing	Text Copying	p	Attention to-Breath
P4/P3	0.99	1.19	.0003	1.01	1.07	.04	1.20
T4/T3	0.77	1.12	.00003	0.75	0.94	.0004	0.88
C4/C3	0.79	1.17	.0003	0.83	1.03	.0006	0.97

*Geometric means over all subjects of EEG power ratios (right/left)

**Significance of differences tested by Wilcoxon Matched-Pair Signed-Ranks Test, all P values two-tailed, ns = .05.

first: higher ratios are found during verbal tasks than during spatial tasks. All three lead pairs show the task-dependent asymmetry in both comparisons (Blocks vs. Write-from-Memory and Text Copying vs. Mirror Drawing).

There are systematic differences between the leads. The parietal leads, in all comparisons in both experiments, exhibit the least task-dependent asymmetry, i.e. the difference in alpha ratio on the verbal task and the spatial task is smaller on the parietal leads than on the temporal and central leads. The temporal and central leads appear to behave similarly in this respect.

The Attention-to-Breath task most closely approximates the conditions under which clinical EEGs are recorded; i.e. little information processing, passive, unstructured. Clinical EEG texts generally state that alpha amplitude is normally higher on the right than the left. We find this to be so for the parietal leads, but consistently reversed for the temporal leads. Table 1-II shows the results from the breathing task of Experiment II. Most subjects have predominant right parietal alpha and predominant left temporal alpha. The central leads show an equal distribution. This reversal between parietal and temporal alpha predominance can also be seen during the active cognitive tasks. (Table 1-I, all tasks except Mental Letter.)

TABLE 1-II

DIFFERENCES BETWEEN ELECTRODE LOCATIONS
IN "RESTING" ALPHA ASYMMETRY

	Parietal	Temporal	Central
Higher Right Alpha	27	9	16
Higher Left Alpha	6	24	15

The functional significance of this reversal of asymmetry is not yet clear, but it precludes classifying a person simply as "right dominant" or "left dominant"; intrahemispheric specialization must be taken into account.

Previous investigators have sought to relate electrophysiological recordings to cognitive functions. A major effort has been devoted to relating the EEG to "intelligence" (29).

Our approach to this problem takes into account three factors which seem to have been neglected in the past.

1. Recording while the subject is engaged in a task rather than trying to relate a "resting" EEG or averaged evoked potential to subsequent performance.

2. Selection of cognitive tasks which clinical evidence has shown to depend more on one hemisphere than the other, and which therefore should be associated with a predictable distribution of brain activity.

3. Selection of electrode placements on clinico-anatomical grounds. A wealth of evidence suggests that temporal and parietal leads should be the most functionally asymmetrical, and occipital leads the most similar. Unfortunately, occipital leads have been used most often in the past, probably because they are not as sensitive to eye movement and muscle artifacts. Usually recordings have been made only unilaterally.

Now that we have established a method for determining lateralization of cognitive function in normal subjects, several major areas of concern can be studied: the generality of lateral specialization of cognitive function in the population, the role of lateral specialization in critical academic skills, the effect of social drugs on hemispheric interaction, and the possibility of training voluntary control over patterns of lateral asymmetry using the feedback EEG.

LATERALIZATION IN LEFT-HANDED AND AMBIDEXTEROUS PEOPLE

The lateralization of cognitive functions described above is characteristic of right-handed people. The cerebral lateralization of left-handed people is more complex. Hecaen (30, 31) has provided an extensive review of the neurological literature and a summary of his own clinical studies and concluded that left-handers show a greater cerebral ambilaterality, not only for language, but also for gnosic and praxic functions. Hecaen distinguishes between left-handedness which is familial and that which follows a perinatal injury to the left hemisphere. The familial type may or may not have reversed language lateralization.

These conclusions were generally confirmed by Satz, et al. (32) in a study of a neurologically normal population. They used the dichotic listening test to assess language lateralization and carefully tested manual superiority rather than relying on the subjects' self-classification as to handedness.

Following the hypothesis of Orton that stuttering and dyslexia can be due to poorly established cerebral specialization (33), many studies have found high incidences of left-handers and ambidexterous people among these clinical groups. Hecaen (31) concludes that while no convincing direct relation has been demonstrated, "disorders of laterality can play a part in a certain number of these cases."

The nature of these "disorders of laterality" is not clear. To our knowledge there have been no attempts to quantitatively evaluate the interaction between the verbal-analytic and spatial-holistic cognitive systems in normal daily activities. Our opinion is that in many ordinary activities normal people simply alternate between cognitive modes rather than integrating them. These modes complement each other but do not readily substitute for each other. Although it is *possible* to process complex spatial relationships in words, it would seem much more efficient to use visual-kinesthetic images. For example, consider what most people do when asked to describe a spiral staircase; they begin using words, but quickly fall back on gesturing with a finger.

Processing in the inappropriate cognitive system may not only be inefficient, but it may actually interfere with processing in the appropriate system. This "interference hypothesis" is supported by a study of left-handed subjects who were presumed to have bilateral language representation (34). Levy compared left-handed and right-handed subjects with equal WAIS verbal scores and found that the left-handers had significantly lower performance scores which she attributed to interference from the presumed ambilaterality of language. Her observation has been confirmed by Miller (35). Similarly, in a group of patients in whom right-hemisphere language was demonstrated with carotid amytal, Lansdell (36) found a negative correlation between language ability and spatial performance scores. Brooks (37) presents additional support for the hypothesis of "interhemispheric interference." Reading a description of spatial relations interferes with the subsequent manipulation of those spatial relations. DenHyer and Barrett (38) demonstrated selective loss of spatial and verbal information in short-term memory by means of spatial and verbal interpolated tasks. Levy has in fact suggested that verbal and nonverbal functions evolved in opposite hemispheres to reduce interference of one system with the other (34).

This evidence of interference between the right and left cognitive modes provides a new kind of support for the hypothesis of Orton: that lack of cerebral lateral specialization plays a major role in dyslexia and stuttering. This hypothesis has continued to sustain interest, in spite of a lack of convincing direct evidence. Until recently, the only generally available index of cerebral lateralization was handedness, and people with little hand preference, or left-handers who were "switched" or those with mixed hand and eye preference were considered to be "high risk." The incidence of such people in clinical categories such as stuttering, dyslexia, and specific learning disability is usually found to be higher than in the normal population.

Our EEG method for studying lateralization of cognitive function, along with the dichotic listening test, can provide a much more direct and presumably more sensitive means for investigating disorders of laterality than measures based on hand, eye, or foot dominance. Our present proposal to extend our measures to left-handed and ambidexterous populations will lay the groundwork for these clinical studies.

BIOFEEDBACK TRAINING FOR VOLUNTARY CONTROL OF EEG ASYMMETRY

Our research has demonstrated characteristic patterns of activity and inactivity for both the verbal and the spatial cognitive modes. It is reasonable to suppose that more selective inhibition and facilitation of each hemisphere can improve performance. It has been shown in many laboratories that when subjects are given exteroceptive feedback on the state of a physiological variable they can learn control of the variable, e.g. EEG alpha, heart rate,

EMG (39, 40, 41). For example, O'Malley and Conners (42) have reported a pilot case of a dyslexic boy who was given lateralized alpha feedback training and showed significant changes in EEG asymmetry. Therefore, with the aid of feedback from our electrophysiological index of cognitive mode, subjects may be able to learn to reduce the interference between hemispheres and thereby improve cognitive performance.

IMPLICATIONS FOR EDUCATION

Our EEG and eye movement studies (26, 43) provide potential methods of assessing an individual's preferred cognitive mode. An individual's preferred cognitive style may facilitate his learning of one type of subject matter — e.g. spatial, relational — and hamper the learning of another type, e.g., verbal analytical. A student's difficulty with one part of a curriculum may arise from his inability to change to the cognitive mode appropriate to the work he is doing.

Studies by Cohen (44), Marsh, et al. (45), and Bogen, et al. (46) have indicated that subcultures within the United States are characterized by a predominant cognitive mode: the middle class is likely to use the verbal-analytic mode; the urban poor is more likely to use the spatial-holistic mode. This results in a cultural conflict of cognitive style and may in part explain the difficulties of the urban poor children in the school system oriented toward the middle class. There seems to be a new recognition among educators of the importance of both modes of experiencing the world (47). Many new programs (e.g. "Sesame Street") emphasize helping verbal-analytically oriented children to develop holistic mode skills as well as helping holistically-oriented children to make use of the traditional verbal-analytic materials. If our project is successful, it may make it feasible to train an individual child to enter both cognitive modes appropriately. With EEG feedback an individual may be able to learn to sustain a pattern of brain activity and the concomitant cognitive mode which is appropriate to reading and arithmetic on the one hand and painting and construction on the other.

Our approach may also be of use in the study of cognitive

development. Since brain injuries before the age of twelve rarely result in permanent aphasia, it is reasonable to suppose that the lateralization of cognitive function is still in flux in young children after the acquisition of speech and even after the acquisition of written language. The maturation of the child's cognitive power may be paralleled by, and perhaps even depend upon, increasing lateral specialization with a resulting decrease in interference between cognitive systems. Our EEG measures of cognitive functioning could be powerful tools for mapping the course of this growth. These measures could be used in diagnosing aberrations in cognitive development. For example, certain forms of dyslexia may be caused by interhemispheric interference. Perhaps "feedback" training to improve selective inhibition of the inappropriate cognitive mode would prove useful in therapy.

REFERENCES

1. Benton, A. L., and Joynt, R. J.: Early descriptions of aphasia. *Arch Neurol, 3*:205-222, 1960.
2. Semmes, J., Weinstein, S., Ghent, L., and Teuber, H. L.: Spatial orientation in man after cerebral injury: I. Analyses by locus of lesion. *J Psychol, 39*:227-244, 1955.
3. Milner, B.: Visually guided maze learning in man: Effects of bilateral, frontal, and unilateral cerebral lesions. *Neuropsychologia, 3*:317-338, 1965.
4. Luria, A. R.: *Higher Cortical Functions in Man.* New York, Basic, 1966.
5. Corkin, Suzanne: Tactually-guided maze learning in man: Effects of unilateral cortical excisions and bilateral hippocampal lesions. *Neuropsychologia, 3*:339-351, 1965.
6. Sperry, R. W., Gazzaniga, M. S., and Bogen, J. E.: Interhemispheric relationships: The neucortical commissures, syndromes of hemisphere disconnection. In Vinkin, P. K., and Bryn, G. W. (Eds.): *Handbook of Clinical Neurology.* Amsterdam, North Holland Publishing Co., 1969, pp. 273-290, vol. IV.
7. Levy, J.: Information processing and higher psychological functions in the disconnected hemispheres of human commissurotomy patients. Unpublished thesis, California Institute of Technology, 1970.
8. Bogen, J. E.: The other side of the brain. *Bull Los Angeles Neurol Soc, 34*:73-105, 135-162, 191, 220, 1969.
9. Levy, J., Trevarthen, C., and Sperry, R. W.: Perception on bilateral chimeric figures following hemispheric deconnexion. *Brain, 95*:61-78, 1972.

10. Nebes, R.: Superiority or the minor hemisphere in commissurotomized man for the perception of part-whole relations. *Cortex, 7*:333-349, 1971.
11. Semmes, J.: Hemispheric specialization: A possible clue to mechanism. *Neuropsychologia, 6*:11-26, 1968.
12. Sperry, R. W.: Hemisphere deconnection and unity in conscious awareness. *Am Psychol, 23*:723-733, 1968.
13. Stent, G.: Prematurity and uniqueness in scientific discovery. *Sci Am,* December, 1972, pp. 84-93.
14. Milner, B.: Brain mechanisms suggested by studies of temporal lobes. In (Eds.): *Language.* New York, Grune, 1965.
15. Kinsbourne, M.: Eye- and head-turning indicates cerebral lateralization. *Science, 176*:539-541, 1972.
16. Critchley, M.: *The Parietal Lobes.* London, E. Arnold, 1953.
17. Humphrey, M. E., and Zangwill, O. L.: Effects of a right-sided occipito-parietal brain injury in a left-handed man. *Brain, 75*:312-324, 1952.
18. Filbey, R. A., and Gazzaniga, M. S.: Splitting the normal brain with reaction time. *Psychon Sci, 17*:335, 1969.
19. McKeever, W. F., and Huling, M.: Left cerebral hemisphere superiority in tachistoscopic work recognition performance. *Percept Mot Skills, 30*:763-766, 1970.
20. Kimura, D.: Cerebral dominance and the perception of verbal stimuli. *Can J Percept, 15*:166-171, 1961.
21. Buchsbaum, M., and Fedio, P.: Visual information and evoked responses from the left and right hemispheres. *Electroencephalogr Clin Neurophysiol, 26*:266-272, 1969.
22. Wood, C., Goff, W. R., and Day, R. S.: Auditory evoked potentials during speech perception. *Science, 173*:1248-1251, 1971.
23. Morrell, L. K., and Salamy, J. G.: Hemispheric asymmetry of electrocortical responses to speech stimuli. *Science, 174*:164-166, 1971.
24. Vella, E. J., Butler, S. R., and Glass, A.: Electrical correlate of right hemisphere function. *Nature (Lond), 236*:125-126, 1972.
25. McAdam, D. W., and Whitaker, H. A.: Language production: Electroencephalographic localization in the normal human brain. *Science, 172*:499-502, 1971.
26. Galin, D., and Ornstein, R.: Lateral specialization of cognitive mode: An EEG study. *Psychophysiology, 9*:412-418, 1972.
27. McKee, G., Humphrey, B., and McAdam, D.: Scaled lateralization of alpha activity during linguistic and musical tasks. *Psychophysiology,* in press.
28. Doyle, J. C., Ornstein, R., and Galin, D.: Lateral specialization of cognitive mode: II. EEG frequency analysis. *Psychophysiology,* 1973, in press.
29. Vogel, W., Broverman, D. M., and Klaiber, E. L.: EEG and mental abilities. *Electroencephalogra Clin Neurophysiol, 24*:166-175, 1968.
30. Hecaen, H., and Ajuriaguerra, J. de: *Left-handedness, Manual Superiority, and Cerebral Dominance.* New York, Grune, 1964.
31. Hecaen, H., and Sauguet, J.: Cerebral dominance in left-handed subjects.

Cortex, 7:19-48, 1971.

32. Satz, P., Achenbach, K., and Fennell, E.: Correlations between assessed manual laterality and predicted speech laterality in a normal population. *Neuropsychologia,* 5:295-310, 1967.

33. Orton, S. T.: Some studies in language function. *Res Publ Assoc Res Nerve Ment Dis,* 13:614-632, 1934.

34. Levy, J.: Possible basis for the evolution of lateral specialization of the human brain. *Nature (Lond),* 224:614-615, 1969.

35. Miller, E.: Handedness and the pattern of human ability. *Br J Psychol,* 62:111-112, 1971.

36. Lansdell, H.: Verbal and non-verbal factors in right hemisphere speech. *J Comp Physiol Psychol,* 69:734-738, 1969.

37. Brooks, L. R.: An extension of the conflict between visualization and reading. *Q J Exp Psychol,* 22:91-96, 1970.

38. DenHyer, K., and Barrett, B.: Selective loss of visual information in short-term memory by means of visual and interpolated tasks. *Psychon Sci,* 25:100-102, 1971.

39. Nowlis, D., and Kamiya, J.: Control of EEG alpha rhythms through auditory feedback and the associated mental activity. *Psychophysiology,* 4:476-484, 1970.

40. Budzynski, T. H., Stoyva, J., and Adler, C.: Feedback-induced muscle relaxation: Application to tension headaches. *J Behav Ther Exp Psychiatry,* 1:205-211, 1970.

41. Hniatow, M., and Lang, P.: Learned stabilization of cardiac rate. *Psychophysiology,* 1:330, 1965.

42. O'Malley, J. E., and Conners, C. K.: The effects of unilateral alpha training on visual evoked responses in a dyslexic adolescent. *Psychophysiology,* 9:467-470, 1972.

43. Kocel, K., Galin, D., Ornstein, R., and Merrin, E. L.: Lateral eye movement and cognitive mode. *Psychonom Sci,* 27:223-224, 1972.

44. Cohen, R. A.: Conceptual styles, culture conflict and non-verbal tests of intelligence. *Am Anthropologist,* 71:826-856, 1969.

45. Marsh, J. F., Tenhouten, W. D., and Bogen, J. E.: A theory of cognitive functioning and social stratification. Progress Report O.E.O. contract. Riverside, Department of Sociology, University of California, 1970.

46. Bogen, J. E., DeZure, R., Tenhouten, W. D., and Marsh, J. F.: The other side of the brain: IV. The A/P ratio. *Bull Los Angeles Neurol Soc,* 37:49-61, 1972.

47. Bruner, J.: *On Knowing: Essays for the Left Hand.* New York, Atheneum, 1965.

Chapter 2

BIOLOGICAL BASIS OF AGGRESSIVE BEHAVIOR: CLINICAL ASPECTS

GEORGE BACH-Y-RITA

W HEN confronted by an assaultive or violent patient, the psychiatrist has at his disposal a variety of approaches, diagnostic possibilities, and treatment modalities. Not surprisingly most of our theoretical framework is strongly biased towards the intrapsychic or towards the study and manipulation of social phenomena. These approaches have been used almost to the total exclusion of other possible causes of aberrant behavior. Although these have unquestionable value, they are by definition limited, particularly when the problem involves more than a learned or neurotic pattern of behavior.

To limit interest to the intrapsychic or social phenomena when attempting to care for the abnormally or habitually aggressive patient is to ignore the role of normal aggression and the abnormal triggering of aggressive responses that may result from impaired cerebral function. It should come as no surprise that the brain, the organ of behavior, like other organs of the body is subject to insult and injury and may malfunction as a result of disease. This malfunction may lead to hyperaggressive behavior.

Most of us who have worked in psychiatric institutions, even for short periods of time, have observed what happens when a physician forgets that the brain is the organ of behavior. Although largely unpublished, we are all familiar with the "depressed" or the "schizophrenic" patient who did not respond to treatment and subsequently died of a brain tumor, was found to be hypothyroid, or had one of a variety of medical illnesses. Even more common is to observe the garrulous or aggressive behavior that frequently occurs following brain surgery trauma or is encountered in the patient with encephalitis. Although it is the

24

neurologist or neurosurgeon who is most likely to see these patients, psychiatrists who have consulted on a neurological service are also likely to observe them. What is most important is that this behavior when observed in a patient known to have suffered recent trauma, etc., is immediately recognized and the behavior is seen as the pathological triggering of what is probably a normal brain mechanism. Some of this has been documented by Malmud (1) who has found that a high proportion of patients with intracranial tumors of the lymbic system have histories that include assaultiveness.

What is surprising is that a psychiatrist seeing a patient with a history of head injury or encephalitis five or ten years after his injury or illness is loath to consider the old brain insult in formulating his differential diagnosis.

History provides some lessons that the physician too often ignores. Rabies, a viral insult to the brain with its characteristic negri bodies in the temporal lobe, is named after one of the primary symptoms of the disease. The word itself is derived from the Latin *rabidus* "to rage," a word itself probably derived from the Sanskrit *rabhas* which means violence or force. For generations it has been recognized that this disease of the brain manifests itself with a characteristic change in behavior, rage.

The reluctance to recognize or even consider biological factors in the care of the habitually violent patient at times verges on the ludicrous.

I was recently asked to consult on a patient charged with a serious crime. In taking a history, I found that this patient had been in and out of prison on several occasions and in jail on numerous occasions. Most of his convictions stemmed from his aggressive or impulsive behavior. When I saw him, he was in his mid-thirties, had been seen by a number of physicians including several psychiatrists, and had an extensive documented medical history.

In taking a history, I found that this man had suffered what was described as "polio" as a very young child and that his youth was punctuated by temper trantrums, fighting, and antisocial behavior. As a young adult, he had numerous conflicts with the law and was in and out of juvenile detention facilities, jail, and finally prison.

At one point his behavior in prison was so bizarre that the guards took note, and he was sent to a neurosurgeon. Following a clearly abnormal electroencephalogram compatible with a diagnosis of temporal lobe disease, the neurosurgeon wisely performed a pneumoencephalogram. This was clearly abnormal with moderate cortical atrophy in the left hemisphere.

The psychiatrist treating him and responsible for his care in the institution where these examinations were performed stuck to his diagnosis of "antisocial personality." Subsequent physicians agreed with the diagnosis of antisocial personality, and the patient was discharged sometime later essentially untreated (except for group psychotherapy), unchanged, and of course to repeat his criminal behavior.

When I saw this patient ten years later, he again had an abnormal electroencephalogram, was disturbed by his own behavior, and described numerous episodes of loss of control and consciousness, and impulsive, assaultive behavior. He was awaiting prosecution for one of these assaults. The final tragedy in the whole case was that at the time of trial, psychiatrists appeared who were willing to swear that they could find nothing wrong with this patient. He was convicted and returned to prison.

This case is a good example of the type of patient with more than a hot temper or the victim of social injustice. He is an example of a particular group of patients nicely described by Meninger (2) as a patient suffering from the third order of dyscontrol or episodic dyscontrol. The psychiatric nomenclature tends to classify these patients either as explosive personalities, psychopaths, or as antisocial personalities. Unfortunately these terms are too often used in a pejorative sense, thereby losing much of their validity and often depriving a patient of a proper examination.

Aggression and/or violence are not abnormal phenomena. On the contrary, aggressive behavior is highly adaptive, and the ability to be physically assaultive and at times to kill remains necessary for the survival of the species. Kenneth Moyers (3) has described several different types of normal aggressive behavior in animals and discusses their role in the process of survival. Some of the types of aggressive behavior that Moyers has described are applicable to man. He lists among them irritable, fear-induced, predatory, maternal, intermale, and instrumental. The clinical problem is to discriminate normal and appropriate aggression from the abnormal.

THE ENDOCRINE CONTROL OF AGGRESSION

Folklore provides a very graphic introduction to the relationships between brain physiology and normal aggressive behavior and the endocrine system. For centuries men have taken animals while they were young and castrated them, thus making the calf become a docile ox instead of an aggressive fighting bull. This is one of the more obvious physiological mechanisms involved in the regulation of aggressive behavior, and particularly intermale aggression.

The effects of gonadal steroids on aggressive behavior have been systematically documented, and it has been demonstrated that estradiol inhibits completely the manifestation of combativeness in isolated male mice. In castrated isolated mice, aggressiveness was readily induced by testosterone (4).

The gonadal hormones are not the only ones involved in the control of aggressive behavior. Sigg (5) presented data which suggests that other hormonal systems in addition to the gonadal hormones contribute to the aggressive response, and Kostowski (6) demonstrated that hydrocortisone significantly increased aggressive behavior in rats. Although research on the effects of hormones on aggression has generally been restricted to the gonadal hormones, there is a growing body of evidence that the pituitary adrenal hormones have a direct correlation.

Parenthetically, Dalton (7) noted that women have a much higher incidence of crime just before and during menstruation. Her observations are yet to be corroborated in groups of aggressive women.

NEUROPHYSIOLOGICAL MECHANISMS OF AGGRESSION

Research on the neurophysiological mechanisms involved in

the display of rage first began with the famous work of Bard (8), who in 1928 demonstrated that in decorticate cats spontaneous or provoked rage requires the presence of the hypothalamus. At that time it was called *sham rage.* In the years following, it became quite clear that the hypothalamus was intimately involved in the mechanisms that when activated (9) produced a behavioral pattern characteristic of rage. The prevalent theories of the time, that higher cortical functions controlled or inhibited subcortical mechanisms, appear to have led to the later studies of Kluver and Bucey (10) in which they found that the bilateral removal of the amygdala in monkeys produced, among other things, tranquility. Some of the work has been applied to humans by Sano (11) who has lesioned the hypothalamus of assaultive brain-damaged children as a means of reducing their assaultiveness.

Stimulation experiments have produced even more information on the physiology of aggressive behavior, and the technique has been particularly well refined by Jose Delgado of Yale University. As revealing as they are, the topic is really too extensive to be reviewed here. Suffice to say that stimulation in animals of several areas including the amygdala, the hypothalamus septum, and the reticular formation can produce what might be interpreted as aggressive or rage-like behavior.

Ursin (12) provides an excellent review of the literature on stimulation and ablation studies of the temporal lobe in animals and humans. The paper discusses which temporal lobe structures are important for those emotional patterns of behavior that we know as anger and fear. Delgado (13) has demonstrated that intracerebral stimulation is best done in the freely moving animal while in an animal colony. He points out that what might be interpreted as aggressive or rage-like behavior by the experimenter is not always seen as such by the other animals in the colony. Aggression being a social response, it requires a suitable target and social setting. It is also influenced by sensory feedback as well as the position of the stimulated animal in the hierarchical order of the colony.

Fighting can be induced by stimulation of the medial hypothalamus of the cat and has been observed by Delgado to result in a series of responses which the investigator could easily interpret as dangerous but which other cats ignore. The response included displaying the teeth, piloerection, and pupilary dilitation. Other cats in the same cage with the stimulated animals did not repond to this in the slightest. Humans, like cats, respond to an aggressive display only in context. An example is the response to aggressive behavior in a three-year-old boy and the response to aggressive behavior in a fifteen-year-old. The first is dealt with at home and is often ignored or seen as mischievious, but when the boy grows and reaches adult size or obtains really destructive skills, the danger potential is recognized and a totally different response is elicited.

A similar phenomena occurs with the explosively aggressive woman. A woman who repeatedly attempts to beat her husband usually gets hurt. A man who repeatedly attempts to beat his wife is likely to get arrested. The woman is usually arrested only if she uses a weapon or if her behavior should lead to injury.

A considerable amount of the work previously done in animals has been reproduced in man, and currently there is rich literature on brain stimulation and aggression in man. It has become quite clear that stimulating the amygdala can produce either anger, rage, or aggression, or more medial stimulation can result in tranquility. Delgado in 1969 stimulated the amygdala and reproduced the rage reactions that occurred in a woman with postencephaletic brain damage and temporal lobe epilepsy (14). This involved a radio-controlled system which permitted stimulation and recording at a distance. Mark and Ervin (15) describe several cases in which stimulation of the amygdala resulted in rage reactions.

A final point is that variations in blood sugar have been demonstrated to be related to irritable aggression, and I have seen a patient with a history of repeated outbursts which included aggressive and assaultive behavior treated as a hysteric for four years until she was found to have episodes of hypoglycemia.

The results of study both with animals and with man using a variety of techniques indicate quite clearly that there are definable systems within the brain which organize attack and defense behavior. When activated either artificially, pathologically, or naturally, aggressive behavior will result. In addition the behavior resulting from the activation of these systems can be modified or altered by the environment.

CLINICAL ASPECTS OF AGGRESSIVE PATIENTS

In the psychiatric or the neurologic clinic, one is not likely to encounter the pure cerebral dysfunction as a cause of aggression. In its purest form, the patient with a brain lesion leading to aggressive behavior continues to function in the light of his past experiences — psychological defenses and social environment. Like Delgado's cats and monkeys, the patient's behavior — whether originating from intrapsychic conflict, cerebral dysfunction, social pressure, or learning — usually is present as a mixture of these factors.

The clinical picture reflects not only pathology, but also culture and social class. This holds true for many psychiatric illnesses and should be expected. Some types of aggressive displays are adaptive and thus reinforced, depending on the environment.

In spite of the large volume of information that has been gathered to date on the biological aspects of aggressive behavior in animals, it is only since the early 1940's that there has been any success in linking aggressive behavior in man with disturbed cerebral function. Originally the attempts were made to link what was known as the psychopathic personality and cerebral dysrhythmias. The early investigators found that there were many more abnormal EEG's among convicted criminals, particularly among convicted criminals with a diagnosis of "psychopathic personality," than in the population at large. These observations have been supported over the years, and it appears that habitually aggressive delinquents are more likely to have abnormal EEG's than the general population.

In a study of 1,250 subjects in custody for crimes of violence (16) 333 subjects were randomly selected. Of these, 62 per cent or 206, had a history of habitual physical aggression or explosive rages. The author found that 65 per cent of the habitually aggressive subjects had abnormal electroencephalograms while only 24 per cent of subjects who committed violent crimes, but were not habitually aggressive, had abnormal electroencephalograms. The same author in a previous study found 12 per cent of the population at large had abnormal encephalograms.

When the otherwise normal habitually aggressive subjects were compared with normal subjects who were known to have committed a solitary act of major bodily violence (generally murder or its attempt), it was found that the habitually aggressive had an incidence almost five times greater of abnormal electroencephalograms. The individuals who committed a solitary act of violence had an incidence of abnormal electroencephalograms comparable to the general population.

The clinical picture of the habitually aggressive patient is not the television image of a cold-blooded killer or a gangster. Quite the contrary, they are usually rather tragic figures whose lives are destroyed by chronic impulsivity. Far from being rewarded for their behavior, they loose jobs, family, and friends as a result of their unpredictable behavior.

Impulsivity and paroxysmal episodes of depression, hostility, or rage pervades the lives of many habitually aggressive patients; although the symptom that arouses most attention is the rage and hostility, the depression is just as painful and important for the patients. In a group that I recently studied in a large prison, of sixty-two habitually aggressive men from which the overtly psychotic had been eliminated, one-half had made a suicide attempt.

In this population 61 per cent had suffered a brain concussion prior to age ten. Childhood behavior patterns also revealed what might be viewed as hyperactive or stimulus seeking behavior, and severe impulsivity was generally manifested by puberty. Somewhat suggestive of a brain dysfunction was the frequency of nondrug induced hallucinations with approximately one-third having suffered visual or auditory hallucinations.

Within this population one observation has attracted my attention. Self-mutilation was a very common finding, with 42 per cent having scars from self-inflicted wounds. The finding of eighty to 100 scars of this type was not unusual. The patients in discussing the episodes of mutilation described not feeling pain or feeling minimal pain while they were cutting. This would permit them to cut themselves repeatedly in a very short time span, perhaps indicative of a disturbance in the ability to feel or use tactile information.

This type of behavior has to be distinguished from the manipulative type of self-inflicted wounds often seen in prisons. The manipulative patients rarely have more than a dozen scars.

Of equal importance but difficult to document in a prison population was the clinical impression that many of the patients had reading difficulties and problems of fine motor control. Clearly in this population cultural and environment factors play a powerful role, and the observation will require confirmation and measurement on a free population.

Some additional information which may lead to the source of cerebral dysfunction was a finding that of the sixty-two men, 58 per cent had suffered broken bones prior to the age of ten. Although this figure may speak for a high incidence of stimulus seeking behavior, when viewed in the light of a high incidence of concussions and family histories of considerable strife and physical violence, the possibility that the patients themselves were the victims of childbattering and head injury with subsequent neurological damage becomes very important.

Electroencephalograms were not readily available in the prison which would have been very interesting, but in a previous population of habitually aggressive outpatients, of 130 patients, seventy-nine received EEG's. Thirty-seven of these showed abnormalities on the electroencephalogram. Twenty of the thirty-seven abnormal revealed spikes in the temporal region and the rest asymmetries or other rhythm changes. Of the total population studied, thirteen of 123 patients were found to have undiagnosed temporal lobe epilepsy. Seven more came already diagnosed as temporal lobe epilepsy.

In the total group of 130 patients, there were thirty whose episodes or outbursts appeared almost seizure-like. In this group, loss of contact with the environment was usually evident during the outburst; at times there were automatisms or prodromal symptoms including auras and frequently what appeared to be postictal states characterized by stereotyped symptoms such as depression, fatigue, sleep, or, on occasion, relaxation or elation.

This group also on occasion presented amnesia, dizziness, or altered states of consciousness. Of this subgroup, fifteen received EEG examinations and nine revealed abnormalities. Of the nine, six (or 40%) had electroencephalograms compatible with a diagnosis of temporal lobe epilepsy (17). In addition to the EEG studies already mentioned, we found that arteriograms (sixteen cases) gave little yield. Pneumoencephalograms, on the other hand, were quite useful, and twenty-two patients with electroencephalograms suggestive of temporal lobe epilepsy received pneumoencephalograms of which eight cases revealed abnormal findings. The most frequent finding was dilatation of the temporal horn or of the lateral ventricles. Skull films were virtually useless.

Although the evidence is quite strong that some types of brain injury or disease lead to behavioral problems, including at times violent or aggressive behavior, I have by no stretch of the imagination attempted to imply that all or even most behavior of this type is the result of brain dysfunction. The point stressed here is that some patients with behavioral symptoms do have a malfunctioning brain. The more symptoms that are evident — such as automatism, impaired consciousness, cognitive deficits, stereotyped behavior, motor or perceptual difficulties — the greater the possibility that the behavior is due to a malfunctioning organ. The case becomes stronger when the clinical history reveals that the patient has suffered a head injury, central nervous system insult, or developmental defect.

The implication for including a medical approach as well as a psychological approach in the evaluation of habitually aggressive patients has enormous consequences for both patients and society. Not only does the finding of a brain dysfunction open a line of approach for therapy, but the social implication for the patient can be very great. The finding of a cerebral dysfunction in a patient is likely to lead to treatment and possible quarantine rather than to an interminable cycle of punishment and decay.

I have tried very briefly to review some of the issues and evidence relevant to the study of aggressive behavior in animals and to relate some of my experiences with aggressive patients. Like most of psychiatry, this is just the beginning. One factor makes the study of aggressive behavior different. The ethical question of how the knowledge will be used in the control of behavior is important, but this should not stop research; rather it should make it necessary that research be open to scrutiny for all of us to use and judge.

REFERENCES

1. Malmud, N.: Psychiatric disorders with intra-cranial tumors of the lymbic system. *Arch Neurol, 17:*113-123.
2. Menninger, K.: *The Vital Balance.* New York, Viking, 1967.
3. Moyers, K. E.: Kinds of aggression and their physiological basis. *Behav Biol, 2:*55, 1968.
4. Suchowsky, G. K., Pegrassi, L., and Bonsignori, A.: The effect of steroids on aggressive behavior in isolated male mice. In *Aggressive Behavior.* New York, Wiley, 1969.
5. Sigg, E. B.: Relationship of aggressive behavior to adrenal and gonodal function in male mice. In *Aggressive Behavior.* New York, Wiley, 1969, pp. 143-149.
6. Kostowski, W., Rowerski, W., and Piechocki, T.: Effects of some steroids on aggressive behavior in mice and rats. *Neuroendocrinology, 6:*311-318, 1970.
7. Dalton, K.: Menstruation and crime. *Br Med J,* December 30, 1961, pp. 1752-1753.
8. Bard, P.: A diencephalic mechanism for the expression of rage with special references to the sympathetic nervous system. *Am J Physiol, 84:*490, 1928.
9. Ranson, S. W.: Some functions of the hypothalamus. *The Harvey Lectures.* Baltimore, Williams & Wilkins, 1937.
10. Kluver, H., and Bucy, P. C.: Preliminary analysis of functions of temporal lobes in monkeys. *Arch Neurol Psychiatry, 42:*979-1000, 1939.
11. Sano, K., Yoshioka, M., Ogashiwa, M., Ishijima, B., and Ohye, C.: Posteriormedial hypothalotomy in the treatment of aggressive behavior. *Confin Neurol, 27:*164-167, 1966.
12. Ursin, H.: The temporal lobe substraight of fear and anger. *Acta Psychol Neurol (Scand), 35:*378-396, 1960.
13. Delgado, J. M. R.: Offensive defensive behavior in free monkeys and chimpanzees induced by radio stimulation of the brain. In Garattini, S., and Sigg, E. B. (Eds.): *Aggressive Behavior.* Amsterdam, Excerpta Medical Foundation, pp. 109-119.
14. Delgado, J. M. R., Mark, V., Sweet, W., Ervin, F., Weiss, G., Bach-y-Rita, G., and Hagiwara, R.: Intra-cerebral radio-stimulation and recording in completely free patients. *J Nerv Ment Dis,* 1968.
15. Mark, Vernon H., and Ervin, Frank R.: *Violence and the Brain.* New York, Har-Row, 1970.

16. Williams, D.: Neuralfactors related to habitual aggression. *Brain, 92*:503-520, 1969.
17. Bach-y-Rita, G., Lyon, J. R., Climent, C. E., and Ervin, F. R.: Episodic dyscontrol: A study of 130 violent patients. *Am J Psychiatry, 127*:1473-1478, 1971.

Chapter 3

DRUG EFFECTS ON
BRAIN PLEASURE MECHANISMS

Hardin B. Jones

Sensual drugs can cause a variety of changes in brain function. The changes range from a sense of intoxication to a sense of clear-headedness, partial simulations of various pleasures, and related alterations of mood and depletion of brain functions. The sensations observed are pleasurable, but these same drugs can cause unpleasant sensations as well, and only pleasurable effects lead to repetitive use. All of these sensual drugs alter functional control mechanisms of the autonomic nervous system extensively. This is so prominently the case, as is evident in the rough division of drug types by whether they largely augment the sympathetic (uppers or stimulant drugs) or parasympathetic (downers or depressant drugs) control centers, that we may presume that an essential part of the sensual effects of these substances is alteration of the sensory modulating activities of the regulative centers of the autonomic nervous system. These matters are too complex to reduce to a simplistic theory of pleasure, for there appears to be many pleasure mechanisms. Observations on the sensual drugs, however, give new clues both as to how pleasure may be induced and how the brain may function in regard to the pleasure principle.

The Weber-Fechner law guides us to comprehend *proportional* differences over the range of sensory functions. For example, the ranges in sight and sound *exponentially* cascade many orders of magnitude between ability to sense the sun or an explosion to seeing the faint glow of a worm in the dark or hearing the Doppler effect from the flight turn of a small gnat's faint buzz. The principle of relative perception applies in several ways to the kinds of mental change associated with sensual drug abuse. It probably accounts for the common, curious result of doping in that estimation of duration of time and the quantitive sensory judgments of size, speed, and distance may be perceived incorrectly. The difficulty appears to be loss of references; for example the person high on a drug may mistake the gnat for an airplane. It is likely that the gratification mechanisms themselves which are so sensitive to sensual drugs have the prime function of standards by which the brain judges quantities as well as qualities within the vast ranges of exponentially enlarging or diminishing sensory evaluations.

G. T. Fechner was also the scientific proponent of pleasure and pain as prime motivators of behavior and of mental process (1). He wrote approximately (also as quoted by Freud (2)) in 1873: "In so far as conscious impulses always have some relation to pleasure (lust) or unpleasant (unlust), pleasure and unpleasure can be regarded as having a psycho-physical relation ... above the threshold of consciousness ... movement is guided by pleasure or unpleasure ..." (1). Sigmund Freud based his own theories on the principles advanced by Fechner. Freud wrote in *Beyond the Pleasure Principle*: "The facts which have caused us to believe in the dominance of the pleasure principle in mental life also find expression in the hypothesis that the mental apparatus endeavours to keep the quantity of excitation present in it as low as possible or at least to keep it constant." (2) These principles, together with that of the conditioned reflex of Ivan Pavlov, permit us to have a superficial or outward understanding of the nature of mental process without understanding the anatomical and chemical mechanisms responsible for thought, memory, deduction, awareness, and mood. Recently scientists have been able to locate a sufficient number of sites of pleasurable sensation in the limbic region of the mid-brain. The clues are sufficient to postulate several, and perhaps many, separate pleasure mechanisms and to believe that they may comprise the specific limbic system function. But certainly the earlier explorers in behavioral science knew that the brain is guided by motivational mechanisms, and they also observed that these motivations, being powerful and fundamental, must have *stabilizing* characteristics equivalent to reference standards. A corollary is that the motivational mechanisms must be protected from excesses because they are also the brain's "Bureau of Standards." In this regard we must consider the fact that the induction of pleasure through *direct* chemical effects on these mechanisms occurs without the shielding of the stabilizing mechanisms. Adlous Huxley misunderstood the nature of brain functions in postulating that the brain, when doped, allowed unfiltered or raw sensory information to flood the sensorium with novel experiences representing the real world.

In 1954 Aldous Huxley published *The Doors of Perception,* an account of his personal experiences with mescaline and other drugs (3). The essay created a following. Huxley was not the first drug user to "confess" fascinations, but his endorsement of mescaline and drugs in general had appeal: "Although obviously superior to cocaine, opium, alcohol, and tobacco, mescaline is not yet the ideal drug ..." The title, taken from a passage of "Prophesy" by William Blake and the text provided an alien view of perception as opening the mind and freeing it through drugs to know reality. Huxley argued that the mind has a "reducing valve" that keeps it from full function and that drugs allow unreduced sensations: "This is how one ought to see" wrote Huxley of his mescalinized gaze at his "jeweled books ... 'how things really are.' " Huxley did say that "... the man who comes back through the door will never be the same as the man who went out." But he was referring to the educative aspects of the experiences rather than alteration of brain function by conditioning or by chemical trauma. Such romantic views of drug use have not shed light on how they affect the brain.

In early 1965 I became aware of the growing social movement advocating drug use. Most prominent in use then were cannabis, mescaline, and LSD, but the list now includes barbiturates, amphetamines, heroin, and others. I began immediately to study the subject. My investigations included in-depth interviews with drug users from samplings throughout the United States and Viet Nam. My studies include my previous work with users of tobacco and alcohol; 1354 cannabis users, approximately one third of whom used other, more powerful drugs as well; 352 heroin addicts; and users of a variety of other drugs. All these interviews were conducted when the subject was sober for the purpose of gaining information about his subjective sensations and experiences. I observed as much as possible regarding the habits, attitudes, and character of each subject.

The sensual drugs cause more than transient intoxications. They may involve persistent sensory changes and alteration of mental process. Drug users are often remarkable resources of comparative subjective sensual experiences, but a drug user has diminished criteria with which to judge the changes either in his health or personality before and after the commencement of drug use. Except for alcoholics, drug users of all other sensual kinds appear to lack an awareness of the change in themselves brought about by drug abuse but may be aware of changes in their friends. However, each drug user, including users of alcohol, believes that he is a moderate user and that his use is tolerable or harmless. He is likely to rationalize that his situation, i.e. his health, personal relationships, his ability to function, is better than it actually is and that it will not degenerate. Most of them think of the brain as a nonphysiologic entity. The drug user may worry about his lungs, liver, or arm veins but not usually about his brain. In the initial stages of drug use, a user almost always states that he will certainly not venture much beyond his present level of involvement.

The ideas of safety and harmlessness in drugs is usually derived from the pleasure the drugs impart. All drug users report that they use drugs because they "like them." The sense of pleasure seems to diminish or eliminate any sense of present or future harm even if they do notice the difficulties of other users. It is more likely, however, that persistent diminished brain function accounts for both the pleasure of drugs and for the lack of awareness of adverse effects. The effects of the sensual drugs as they are observed by drug users are as follows.

CANNABIS

In my interviews with young cannabis users, it soon becomes apparent that the appeal of this drug is the *good feelings* it induces. Relaxation is often cited, as is the drug's ability to enhance sexual and other sensual pleasure, music, color, touch, etc. It remains to be shown whether such effects are indeed augmentations or the deletions that can be demonstrated in vision and hearing. I think the latter is generally more likely. It does appear that cannabinols concentrate in the limbic region of the mid-brain and that the same region shows atrophy on heavy chronic exposure to cannabis according to the investigations of Campbell, et al. (4). Although no brain function studies were done in the cannabis users I have interviewed, I believe through the experience of many interviews that I can tell roughly the extent of involvement with cannabis from differences in facial muscle movement. Facial muscles reflect the details of mental process in the alert normal. The bright quick expressions of young faces are dulled persistently when they have been using cannabis; the eye movements drift away and snap back with mental gaps caused by the lessened attention span. Some cannabis users are actually bleary in facial expression even though they are not actively intoxicated. Perhaps thoughts are less detailed or perhaps the linkages between thought and facial muscles in many associative centers of the mid-brain are not working well. I believe both are likely explanations. Mid-brain structures are severely damaged in heavy use as found by Campbell, et al. (4), so it is reasonable that even at earlier levels of exposure there may be detectable functional impairment revealed in thought tracking by facial muscles.

The marijuana user often discusses thought formation of intoxication as "stoned" thinking. I characterize this stoned thinking as the use and acceptance of nonsequiturs. Certainly something has gone astray in thought formation to permit this degree of sloth to pass for reason. I hold, however, that this tendency is still detectable, although in a lesser extent when the cannabis user is sober.

Generation of good feeling or enhancement of it by cannabis is probably not different in kind from that induced by alcohol, ether, barbiturates, or other intoxicating drugs. It is my hypothesis that gratification mechanisms, feeling good, are stimulated, and there is a strong association between feeling good and sexual inclination. In the use of alcohol, cannabis, and heroin these sensual states are associated so that at initial use these drugs have reputations as aphrodisiacs. The good feelings fail as sexual capacity fails; with powerful drugs this can be rapid. Perhaps feeling good is a prerequisite step to sexual inclination. With cannabis the feeling is more powerfully generated than in the case of alcohol, and this is in keeping with the fact that the use of cannabis progresses more rapidly in degree of use. The average cannabis user progresses from occasional use to daily use in 3.5 years. The sexual and good feelings associated with heroin is more powerful yet, and with heroin easily available the average user progresses from trial to daily use and addiction in one month.

The occasional use of marijuana may enhance sexual sensation, but my interviews with those who use it several times a day suggest that the effects shift with heavy use from hypersensitivity to numbness and from sexual sensual interest to disinterest. Such a user is comparable to the alcoholic, but he develops more pronounced and earlier sensory deprivation and motor impairment. He does not recognize the gradual reduction of sexual inclination or any of the other effects of his abuse to cannabis, although some users admit to the impairment of memory. It is reasonable to assume that the very increments of mental function that are missing are the ones that are necessary to initiate functions of that sort. Thus the person with a hole in his memory is not aware of it from within. Likewise the person with diminished sexual function has correspondingly reduced inclination, and so he cannot be aware of the missing function until someone challenges him enough to have him remember the change in behavior.

This lack of awareness on the part of the cannabis user is an important symptom of its use. It makes the study of cannabis difficult because it limits the sources of information and the efficacy of interviews. Heroin and cannabis users have in common that they also cannot grasp the significance of their situation. Some mental linkages seem impaired.

In 1969 I began to test the mental status of cannabis users by challenging them to stop using the drug in order to observe the consequent changes. I reasoned that we are unaware of suppression of mental function such as in going to sleep or suffering anoxia, but that in recovery from sleep, the suppression is easily noticed. This theory was validated by the first and subsequent user who agreed to abstain. He had been using cannabis several times a week. The first five weeks of abstinence he noticed no changes, but with the sixth week, his sense of improvement in mental function was dramatic. I have since challenged more than a thousand college students with this proposition: "If you use cannabis, you cannot know whether it has affected you unless you totally abstain for several months. Then you may notice a difference." Most of them are content to believe that cannabis is harmless. If they had any intention of abstaining, it was to prove that I was misinformed. To date, none have returned to make this claim, although 343 have reported marked improvement. Of these, forty-three claimed some degree of mental clarity after two weeks, but most did not notice the marked change until the fifth week or so. The usual description of recovery included memory improvement and clearer thinking. Only six have returned uncertain of any change, but they were not steady users and presumably whould have less recovery to notice. Even so, two of these now at six months are claiming that they really do "feel better." Since the number who were weekend users was 114, the noticeable recovery was not limited to daily users. These observations indicate the cumulative nature of the suppression of mental function by cannabis. Thirteen carefully studied cases of behavioral disorder causatively associated with cannabis were presented October 2, 1971, in the *Journal of the American Medical Association,* by Professors of Psychiatry Kolansky and Moore (5). All of these cases were unable to comprehend personal difficulties even though each became unemployed, deserted family responsibilities, and become indolent. Marked improvement occurred on full abstinence for several months but only in those with less than three years of heavy use.

The novice cannabis users whom I interviewed usually stated they would not use more powerful drugs; yet marijuana smokers with over a year's experience had usually done so. All of the 210

LSD users interviewed as well as all* of the 352 heroin addicts and eighty nonaddicted heroin users stated that they used marijuana before LSD or heroin. It became apparent to me that, in general, those who do not use cannabis will not use LSD or heroin. In my interviews of United States soldiers in Viet Nam who had not used cannabis but who did smoke tobacco, all of them had rejected cigarettes laced with heroin. Those who had smoked cannabis obviously accepted more the heroin cigarette readily, for only cannabis users became heroin users. It appears that the cannabis user acquires deficient judgment perhaps associated with his lack of awareness of the effects cannabis has had on him.

ALCOHOL

Alcohol users who begin with occasional use and who progress to daily use take about fifteen years to reach this stage. It usually takes twenty to thirty years to become involved with the heavy daily use associated with a specific form of alcoholism. The alcoholic uses alcohol because it gives him pleasure and because he claims it is disagreeable to be sober. Many of them say, "It's hell to be sober." I am convinced that this attitude is the result of a functional brain change that is induced by the abuse of alcohol. The change can be viewed as functional failure of natural sources of sensory gratification, a form of sensory deprivation. Alcoholics also progressively develop motor tremor, impaired coordination, and impaired sexual and sensual functions whether they are intoxicated or sober. Sensory correlative functions, motor coordinative functions, and autonomic control centers are weakened. Even with such degrees of brain damage, however, the alcoholic can comprehend his difficulty enough to know that he has a problem. Alcoholics frequently warn others. It must therefore be that alcohol does not affect the same "comprehending" portion of the brain as do cannabis and

---

*Questionnaires to heroin users show a high percentage, usually about 90 per cent, stating prior use of cannabis. I believe the interview method is more likely to get correct information. The types of cases collected are from the drug movement with high association with marijuana. It is also apparent from recent interviews of black prostitute-junkies in New York City that they have little cultural fear of heroin and are likely to use it first if it is available before they use cannabis.

heroin. Users of these drugs at the same level of dependency do not warn others. I believe the reason is that they do not comprehend the problems because of chronic changes in brain function.

Those who use alcohol may have the sensation of clear-headedness, but the sensation develops, especially at a heavy dosage, unmistakably involving mental confusion. The case of the loquacious drunk is well known. The conclusion can be drawn that alcohol induces only the sensation of clear-headedness, and this is an effect of depletion of brain function during acute intoxication. There are severe symptoms in withdrawal from addiction to alcohol, the *delirium tremens,* and these symptoms indicate that there is extensive involvement of the autonomic nervous system with the adjustments for drinking. The alcoholic does not continue to drink out of fear of withdrawal symptoms but from the pleasurable sensations it gives him; in the usual example, the natural powers of good feeling fade simultaneously. As in all heavy drug abuse, pleasure fades with illness; then he becomes intoxicated to keep from feeling bad.

BARBITURATES

Barbiturate users usually reach a state of addiction in a few weeks after beginning with a sensual abuse of sleeping tablets. In the drug culture, users are generally much younger than the adult alcoholic, but they exhibit many of the same effects: sexual inactivity, intermittent use of alcohol or combinations of alcohol and barbiturates, and severe symptoms upon abstinence representing long-extant and long-persisting disturbances in the autonomic nervous system. The barbiturate addict also suffers from an inability to feel good when sober. He too feels that a sober state is painful. Intoxication from both barbiturates and alcohol is regarded as pleasurable, feeling good. Obviously there has been change in the working of pleasure mechanisms so they do not respond positively in the absence of barbiturates. The condition parallels the changes in alcoholism including the substitution of either drug for the other.

STIMULANTS

My subjects described the pleasures of amphetamines as a sense of well-being but quite different from that of the depressant drugs or cannabis. The good feeling is associated with excitement. In further analysis of comments by stimulant users, I am led to postulate that these effects are, from the standpoint of the brain, like preorgasmic sensations as those derived from masturbation. I conclude that the amphetamines (and the similar drug, cocaine) simulate pleasurable mental excitement equivalent to the preorgasmic sexual sensations which are associated with sensory correlative functions and are linked to sympathetic nerve activity.

With amphetamine use, some interviewees report if they attempt to perform the sexual act while under the influence of the drug they cannot reach orgasm. It is only when the effects of the drug have subsided that the climax is possible. This leads to the postulation that the sex act is prolonged by a block of sexual climax. The orgasm depends on a natural burst of sympathetic activity and the abrupt transfer of dominance from the sympathetic to the parasympathetic control centers. This coordination of and transition between the sympathetic and parasympathetic control centers can be observed in the diameter of the pupil during the sex act. It widens slightly in the preorgasmic phase, dilates abruptly at the moment of impending orgasm, and then narrows. The coordinated transition cannot take place when the brain's controls are overwhelmed by the amphetamine stimulation of the sympathetic nervous system. The prolongation of the sex act under the amphetamine, Preludin®, was first reported by Louria (6). This drug was thought to be an aphrodisiac, but it merely postponed the climax by interference with the sensual progression in the sex act.

Amphetamines or cocaine impart a sense of being awake, alert, and clear-headed. Judgment, however, is seriously impaired as evidenced from the acts ranging from harmless impetuosity to murder while "clear-headed" and stimulated. Paranoia is a common mental state associated with this clear-headedness, and when it occurs there is reason to suspect that the brain is being deprived of the balancing forces of reason and sensory input. It is more likely, then, that the sense of hyperawareness is really a deception; the real state is still sensory deprivation. The "speed-freak" is hyperactive and does not have motor impairment to restrict the carrying out of his deluded inclinations. But he does have the sensation of clear-headedness, and he is capable of clear, unslurred communication.

Cocaine sniffers describe their experience euphorically as a clear-headed high. Although amphetamines and cocaine have equivalent effects pharmacologically, the reported sensations experienced with amphetamines by cocaine users, is that cocaine is more purely pleasurable — stimulation without the "muggy" feeling attributed to amphetamines. The person "high" on cocaine, although thinking of himself as clear-headed, responsible, and reasoning, is actually often rash and unreasoning. Obviously the effect involves induction of sensation of clear-headedness but no more the real basis for that realization than the sense of well-being commonly induced by intoxicants.

OPIATES AND HEROIN

Interviews of heroin addicts became easy to arrange because of the increase in heroin use in Berkeley after 1967. Some of the addicts were students. All of the first fifty had been college students up to the beginning of their heavy drug use, and about half of them had come to Berkeley after drug use had become their life-styles. These first interviews provided some interesting facts. The frequency of dosage varied from one to twenty intravenous injections per day; the usual frequency was four times per day; there was a marked reduction in the pleasurable response unless the dosage was progressively increased; all subjects were multiple drug users and had been heavy cannabis users prior to use of heroin; all had taken up the use of each drug in their experience through the advise of a friend; all described the effect of the intravenous "hit" as a rush which, on detailed questioning appeared to be like a sexual orgasmic sensation except that it lasted much longer and ejaculation did not take place. I was not, in these first interviews, aware of the sexual incapacitation of the young men. The needed insight was provided by a couple who stated that to have sex they had to reduce the dosage of heroin, and after a small enough fix to barely abolish withdrawal symptoms, and have sex within the hour. The same day I interviewed a young man who, although a heroin addict, had not been in close touch with the drug culture. His difficulty in trying to eliminate drug use and his failure to do so was his sexual impotence which would not disappear with simple abstinence. In his case sexual activity had diminished rapidly as his use of heroin began, and sexual capacity was gone by the time he knew he was addicted. The young man clearly described the sensation of taking heroin intravenously as equivalent to sexual orgasm. He has linked his impotency, including his inability to have an erection, to heroin addiction. He had panicked when he made this deduction and began to inject himself about ten times a day. Later, another case told me of how he panicked when he discovered he could not get an erection or have sexual sensations. He, too, then injected himself more and more frequently until he reached at least twenty times a day. Both men were hospitalized for a cure, but when their sexual capacity did not return after several weeks of total abstinence, each returned to heroin. They have subsequently, after several tries, returned to normal life through total abstinence. The functional deficiencies blocking deep sleep, sexual functions, feeling good, and the like gradually returned *after* six and eight months of total abstinence.

SUMMARY OF SENSUAL DRUGS AND SEX

It became evident to me that a significant part of the behavioral pattern of addiction could be traced to the close parallel between the sex-like sensations induced by drugs and natural sexual sensations. Other sensual and functional mechanisms were also affected by drugs, but sex was a function with important significance to everyone. Both addiction patterns and normal sexual habits are developed through conditioning to pleasure-giving stimuli. Each drug has its own way of affecting the sexual system, either by enhancing its function or mimicking sexual sensations. Each disrupted sexual functioning, and eventually even the drug failed to produce the quasi-sexual sensations. The patterns of sexual substitutions were as follows:

1. Cannabis as an aid to sex: In acute use it lowers the inhibitions and reportedly enhances sexual sensations. The sensual effects decrease, however, with prolonged use and increased doses.

2. Amphetamines and cocaine in high doses cause preorgasmic sexual sensations with or without actual sexual activity, and they delay or inhibit sexual climax. There is sometimes ejaculation by the male promptly following injection of amphetamines but the preorgasmic phase of sexual sensations continues without transfer to orgasmic phase. Thus, even though stimulants may temporarily prolong erection, they disrupt sexual function. These stimulant drugs seem to act by activating sensual mechanisms responding to the sympathetic nervous system and suggest a working linkage of sympathetic function with the pleasure mechanism possibly in the limbic region.

3. The use of amphetamines for prolonged sensations or hallucinations are often followed by taking a "downer" to avoid the depression of withdrawal from amphetamines. The downers are either barbiturates or opiates. When high doses of amphetamines are injected, then followed by an injection of heroin, the sequence of sex-like events and sensations were ejaculation, preorgasmic sensations lasting several hours, then orgasm without ejaculation upon the injection of heroin. The sensations of this combination are wholly sex-like but occur entirely within the brain and without relationship to the sex organs themselves. Significantly, events related to these sexual sensations are out of sequence: ejaculation takes place before either preorgasmic excitement or climax.

4. Withdrawal from heroin usually causes the reverse from the acute effects on the sexual system, but in this case the result is still confusion of the order of events in the full sexual experience. The person undergoing withdrawal is likely to have spontaneous ejaculation and either premature ejaculation or inability to reach climax if he masturbates. Sexual dreams return, but are often incomplete and made

transitions to a vision of heroin injection instead of natural sexual climax. It appears that some sexual capacities return during detoxification.

5. Heavy barbiturate or alcohol use coincides with sexual inactivity, and there is usually sexual impotency even during periods between intoxication.

HEROIN SMOKING AND CHANGES IN BRAIN FUNCTION PRIOR TO ADDICTION

An opportunity to study drug using soldiers in Viet Nam in October, 1971, and March, 1972, as well as in Germany and Thailand in March, 1973, served to extend my information about the effects of heroin (7). There are some significant differences between junkies who inject less potent heroin and the soldiers in Viet Nam. The soldiers in Southeast Asia usually smoked heroin; those in Germany, like junkies at home, inject heroin to increase the efficiency of the use due to high costs. The effects of smoking are similar to injection in a prolonged sensual rush. Once addicted, a smoker often consumes several grams of heroin a day where a junkie type addict injects from 4 to 100 milligrams daily, divided into about four doses. With allowance for a loss of heroin in the burning of the cigarette, it still appears that the addict smoking heroin in Viet Nam was exposed to considerably more heroin than a mainliner. A prevalent notion in Viet Nam was that the heroin there is nonaddictive because it is relatively pure (90%) but there can be no question of its addictive properties and its ability to give the same rush as injected heroin. Injection of heroin by soldiers, however, was a last resort when the heroin was in short supply.

There was consistent physical and behavioral changes among all the addicted soldiers I interviewed. Although the initial trials of heroin were unpleasant experiences usually marked by nausea, they reported that they felt, from the start of heroin use, especially bad in the morning upon awakening (this was distinctly different than withdrawal; it also represented a *lack of good feeling*). They all had stopped having sexual dreams, and they no longer had morning erections. The men usually continued taking heroin to combat these symptoms and in doing so found an increasing sense of isolation, loneliness, and paranoia. All had stopped writing letters home shortly after the first use of heroin and explained that they no longer felt connected to their homes, family, or friends. The failure to write letters is significant. These soldiers had, in most instances, been active in writing home. The writing filled the time, and they could actively think of home. They were also anxious to receive letters in return. The cessation of writing was abrupt and dramatic. It was also recent enough so that each remembered the change in attitude. The few questioned about receipt of letters also made it clear that they would, after heroin usage began, allow letters to accumulate unopened. I found no more implicit measure of the fact that heroin causes an immediate and long-lasting mental change reducing interpersonal relationships. This effect is not due to acute use of heroin, for these soldiers were not acutely involved most of the time prior to addiction. (The average time from first use to addiction in those addicted was one month.)

Approximately half of the heroin-using soldiers who were interviewed had persistent sexual incapacitation lasting for several days following the first use of heroin. Some of them who were from the beginning using heroin every few days were essentially incapacitated sexually from the first use. The first knowledge of sexual incapacitation by heroin-using soldiers was likely going with their buddies to prostitutes and finding that they could not erect the penis. The other half of those taking heroin and in the preaddiction stages of heroin use could achieve erection but could not reach the sexual climax even though coitus might last for several hours. Both types were fully sexually incapacitated by the time they were addicted to heroin.

In the heroin user, the loss of sexual powers, of good feelings, of morning erection and of sexual dreams, all of which occur before true addiction, points to the significant changes caused by the drug in the brain's associative pathways of pleasure. In addition, the disturbances of many psychic functions and urinary and bowel functions indicate a profound degree of functional interplay in the normal brain between conscious process, the pleasure processes, and the regulative controls of the autonomic nervous system whose controls are located so close to the pleasure mechanism of the limbic region. The extent of the changes in the function of the brain caused by heroin is indicated by the fact that persistent functional disturbances not only precede true addiction but appear to continue long past withdrawal symptoms.

It appears that suppression of various natural sensations of pleasure ranging from friendly communications with others to the personal inward sense of well-being are suppressed by the taking of heroin. The suppression tends to persist and to occur in the initial stage of use. The suppression of capacity for pleasure and gratification precedes the attainment of pleasure and gratification from the taking of heroin. Thus it is not likely true that the heroin experience transcends normal ranges of pleasurable experiences; it is merely that, by relative contrast to the sensory deprivation induced by heroin, sensations induced by heroin appear to be greater.

EFFECTS OF CANNABIS AND HEROIN
ON MEMORY AND COMPREHENSION

Still other changes in behavior affect the drug user as observed especially in heroin or heavy cannabis use. They forget; which is to say their memory functions are impaired. They also cannot comprehend the significance of their situation (7). It is tempting to say that both of these characteristics may represent a difficulty of transfer from the short- to the long-term memory which has been described for cannabis (8). A drug user can know about his difficulties but cannot comprehend them. The heroin addict, as I have said, knows he is sexually incapacitated, but rarely seeks help or advise; the cannabis user does not really understand his altered mental functions, yet he may admit that he has changed in behavior and attitude. The close anatomical linkages between what is known of location of memory and pleasure mechanisms together with a necessary linkage between memory and conditioned response suggest that memory plays an important role in the mechanisms of pleasure.

THE PLEASURE MECHANISMS

The above data compiled from the reports of drug users has led to postulations that drugs activate the pleasure mechanisms either through stimulation or chemical mimicry. The brain then readjusts its pathways to function in the presence of the drug so that functions governed both through the autonomic nervous system and in conscious process are altered. Early use of heroin, before addiction, clearly shows that pleasure mechanisms are already dimmed. It is not that heroin is more pleasurable but that *normal pleasures are persistently suppressed from the beginning of doping.* The form of sensory deprivation induced by the sensual drugs causes persistent suppression of pleasurable awareness. Perhaps this is because the natural pleasure pathways are reconditioned to respond only to drugs. In heavy drug abuse, they are traumatized, for they do not respond to drugs either, and they may not recover. Sensual drug action can interfere with sensory information to such a degree as to cause numbness, but more often the effect is on the sensations derived from the primary senses. Sensory information can reach consciousness, but the drug user's sense of pleasure now is associated with alternations in sensory correlative functions, and these form his understanding of pleasure. The drug user lacks responses to external stimuli except as in taking drugs. Even the most powerful drives and their pleasure-mechanism incentives are perverted to the drug experience: *interest* in and capacity for sex, hunger and its satisfaction, fatigue and sleep, bladder and bowel sensations and controls, and the need for positive response to and satisfaction from people, friends, and family. The perversions of these instincts are noted dramatically in the heroin user, but they are still detectable trends in the paranoia and sensory deprivation associated with all sensual drug abuse. They may also account for the "depersonalization" noted by Kolansky and Moore in persons who have been heavy users of cannabis.

The kinds of pleasure mechanisms are described in relation to kinds of sensations, and some of them, as described by Heath, are located anatomically by probing and stimulating parts of the midbrain (9). Many correspond to sensations at a visceral or sexual level. When we fill what's empty, empty what's full, and scratch what's itching, the brain receives appropriate rewards of pleasure. The mechanisms for feeling good, clear-headed, friendly, and the like are influenced by drugs; the malfunction of them is a part of the pattern of sensory deprivation caused from drug abuse.

Reflex functionings of the brain appear to be arranged so that the pleasure mechanisms are the standards against which consciousness searches for approval or disapproval. These pleasure standards, conditioned by experience and held beyond the range of the conscious process, constitute the only rewards we can know. They are easily disturbed by chemical stimulation. When DeQuincey wrote on his initial discovery of the pleasures of opium eating: ... "happiness might now be bought for a penny, and carried in the waistcoat pocket," he had no insight yet to deprivation of happiness he would suffer through opium-eating. There can be no doubt that the sensual reward mechanisms can be weakened by the sensual drugs.

Intellectual types of pleasure sensations exist and illusion of them is also induced by drugs. These illusions are sensations of understanding *without a factual basis*. William James wrote of the semiconscious states of inhalation of ether or nitrous oxide (which, in my opinion, have fully the same witnesses in current users of the hallucinatory drugs): "Depth beyond depth of truth seems revealed to the inhaler. This truth fades out, however, or escapes, at the moment of coming to and if any words remain over..., they prove to be the veriest nonsense. Nevertheless, the sense of a profound meaning having been there persists..." (11)

HALLUCINATION

Although I will not attempt an analysis of the actual mechanism affected in hallucination, the experience indicates that the effect is interference with sensory correlative mechanisms. The normal sensory correlative functions in the example of vision are: to stabilize the field seen by taking out motion due to eye movement; to detect real movement by objects in the view or relative to the body; to establish depth and perspective; to put the color where it is supposed to be because color is not evenly detected over the retina; to correct for minor mechanical defects such as astigmatism, focus, and holes in the retina; to correlate sight with equilibrium, hearing, and memory; and the pulling together of the three segments of the retina which reach the visual centers by different nerve pathways. The normal brain really sees "how things really are" even though the eyes do not. The facts of vision are the opposite of the Huxley deductions when under the influence of mescaline (3).

The hallucinatory aberration of color, color distribution, motion in the field of vision, indistinct separations of objects, are all easily explained as failures of the visual correlative functions. The seeing of things that aren't there, not seeing things that are there, and the fusing together of objects appears to be due to deletions in the field of vision, actual holes which cannot be seen because the brain either picks up the continuity from the other side of the hole or fills in from memory. The distortions of other senses are analogous to visual hallucination whereby the sensory correlative centers either fail to complete the correlative of a sensation or they fill in absent sensory data with information stored in the memory.

In those having persistent effects from LSD, the problems are not solely flashbacks but are ruminations on these experiences so that they compete for attention. There is also the matter that some mental experiences in the form of revelations are impressed deeply into the memory beyond the capacity of immediate reasoning to set straight. Often these disturbances, based on powerful illusions, involve religious experiences. But they may be Satanic as well as related to the positive religion normal to that person.

Religion and Drugs

Large numbers of drug users have found that in conversion to and exercise of religion there are satisfactions greater than the drug experiences. My case histories of such persons indicate that drug use diminishes and finally stops as they respond to the new source of satisfaction and the new peer pressure against the use of drugs. The exception in this instance is in the Satanic forms of religion; they are not healing and they do not free the person from drug dependency.

I have collected twenty-seven cases of persons who have had a spectacular spiritual experience involving Christian religious conversion and simultaneous relief from involvement with drugs. They all had in common a greed for sensual experience, drug addiction of a severe form, severe sensory deprivation, and illness giving a premonition of death. At the moment of praying, they had a sensation of light from within the head. Afterward, they all had full and rapid recovery of sensual functions, including sexual functions, without withdrawal symptoms. The interesting phenomena of light is from inside the visual correlative centers and is a sign that the paranoia and severe sensory deprivation is suddenly lifted. These cases and the more commonly encountered person who has found comfort in religion are an indication that whatever the nature of the sensations of joy or pleasure that are associated with religion, they are not damaged by drug abuse as are the sensual mechanisms, and more importantly, this form of joy is able to reactivate the sensual functions. The possibility exists that the mental life from religion may generally elevate feelings of well-being and related pleasure mechanisms somewhat in reverse of the deprivation of these sensations brought about by drug abuse. Several abstaining heroin addicts still affected by sensory deprivation have told me that they were tempted to try religion because religious music caused them to have "a stir of feeling inside." The long association of religion with rehabilitation of addicts is well-known in the work of the Salvation Army, Alcoholics Anonymous, and other organizations. It is also evident as a help in drug rescue efforts involving rehabilitation of any kind of sensual drug dependency.

CONCLUSIONS

1. In spite of the notions that the sensual drugs enable a person to reach higher, altered states of consciousness, evidence indicates that the brain under the influence of these drugs is in fact denied the full use of mental powers.

2. The sensations from sensual drugs commonly involves various pleasurable sensations and especially the sense of well-being. These effects seem to be due to chemical titillation of the pleasure mechanisms. In each known effect, to the degree of pleasure and the duration of experience, the natural function of the mechanism is dimmed. This leads to a form of sensory deprivation of derived sensations in the capacity to feel good, in the function of the sexual system, and in the domain of interpersonal responses. The brain essentially tricks one into believing all is well when actually, for his own health and safety, he should perhaps be responding otherwise.

3. The experiences of stimulant drugs and of some forms of alcoholic intoxication do not lead to a genuine increase of mental powers but to the sensation that the brain is clear-headed. Sense of clear-headedness appears to be one of the sensual experiences.

4. The sexual similarities of the sensual drugs stem from the fact that the stimulants mimic the preorgasmic phase of sex, whereas the depressant drugs mimic the orgasmic phase. No stimulant or depressant drug, or combination thereof, is capable of enhancement of the full sex act or reduplication of the sequence of sensations of the sex act. That depends on an intricate balance between the sympathetic and parasympathetic control centers.

5. Brain changes induced by drugs include the lack of ability to comprehend the degree of change. It appears that the very parts of the brain that are perturbed are the ones most needed to comprehend the degree of loss.

6. Sensual drugs excite or inhibit pathways through the brain creating functional disturbances throughout the brain from the controls of the autonomic nervous system to the higher levels of memory, association, and reason. These disturbances begin before true addiction is established and persist even after withdrawal and detoxification.

7. The pleasure from drugs is relatively magnified by comparing drug sensations with the feeble or absent natural

function of gratification mechanisms injured through drug abuse.

REFERENCES

1. Fechner, G. T.: Einige Ideen zur Schopfungs-und Entwicklungsgeschichte der Organismen, 1873 (Part XI, Supplement, 94).
2. Freud, Sigmund: *Beyond the Pleasure Principle* (translation by Strachewand and Zilboorg). New York, Liveright, 1959. Originally *Jenseits Des Lustprinzips.* Leipzig, Vienna and Zurich, Internationale Psychoanlyticher Verlag, 1920.
3. Huxley, Aldous: *The Doors of Perception* New York, Har-Row, 1954.
4. Campbell, A. M. G., Evans, M., Thomson, J. L. G., and Williams, M. J.: Cerebral atrophy in young cannabis smokers. *Lancet,* 2:1219-1924, 1971.
5. Kolansky, Harold, and Moore, Wm. T.: Toxic effects of chronic marihuana use *JAMA, 222:*35-41, 1972.
6. Louria, Donald: *The Drug Scene.* New York, McGraw, 1968.
7. Jones, Hardin B.: A report on drug abuse in the Armed Forces. *Vietnam Medical Service Digest,* The United States Air Force, August, 1972, pp. 25-36.
8. Drachman, David A., and Hughes, John R.: Memory and the hippocampal complexes. *Neurology, 21:*1014, 1971.
9. Heath, Robert G.: Pleasure response of human subjects to direct stimulation of the brain: Physiologic and psychodynamic considerations. In *The Role of Pleasure in Behavior.* New York, Har-Row, 1964.
10. DeQuincy, Thomas: *Confessions of an English Opium Eater.* New York, Lupton, 1899.
11. James, William: *The Varieties of Religious Experiences.* New York, Longmans & Green, 1902.

Chapter 4

THE PYRAMIDAL TRACT
IN PHYLOGENY

Gerhardt von Bonin

The pyramidal tract comprises those fibers which go through the medulla oblongata to the spinal cord.

It is clear by now that almost all the fibers arise in the cortex, although not all of the fibers go to the spinal cord (1). The only exception seems to be a few fibers (about 4%) which go from the cord to the cortex.

We ought to say a few words about the structure of the cortex, the horizontal layering of which is so obvious that a great deal of work has been spent on it (2, 3, 4, 5, 6, 7). Generally six layers are recognized of which the first (they are counted from the surface to the depth) is almost free of cell bodies, but contains numerous synapses between axons and dendrites of cells whose bodies are in lower layers or in other parts of the brain. The second layer contains numerous small cells, the third is composed of somewhat wider spaced cells, many of which are of the pyramidal variety. The fourth is generally densely filled with small cells, the fifth is variable but generally contains wider spaced large pyramidal cells which in some areas attain giant size. In the precentral region they are known as cells of Betz, and their axons become pyramidal fibers. The sixth layer contains polymorph cells which are fairly densely arranged. The subdivision into fields is in some places very obvious, in others rather subtle. This is very clear in the central region: precentrally is the thick, agranular cortex with the giant cells of Betz; postcentrally is the thin koniocortex. But it is unnecessary for our purpose to elaborate that line further.

Of far greater importance, at least at the present time, is the arrangement of the cortical cells in vertical columns, as the physiological experiments of Mountcastle, Hubel, and Wiesel and the anatomical studies of Szentagothai and others have made clear (8, 9, 10, 11).

In properly cut sections this arrangement can be seen everywhere. Each column contains about ten cells at a given level, and the columns are about 2 to 400μ apart from each other, arranged in fairly regular hexagons. In the somesthetic region which interests us here, each column appears to receive impulses of only one kind. I say appears because most columns are slightly bent and the probing electrode must of necessity go down straight.

The sense of touch depends in its efficiency largely on the movements of that part of the body which does the touching (12). This makes the intimate connection of the motor and sensory part of the cortex easily understandable. In the opossum, motor and sensory cortex largely overlap (13, 14) while in man there is a clear separation of the two (15). This, of course, does not mean that there is no connection between motor and sensory cortex, but the separation is obvious. There are U-fibers between the motor and the sensory area, and there are other fibers which go from area 6 to the parietal region so there is ample occasion for integration between motor and sensory impulses.

Whether it is quite fair to compare the opossum, a marsupial, with man, who belongs to the eutheria, is doubtful, for in all eutheria the motor and the sensory homunculus (sit venia verbo) is represented in the cortex in such a way that the two ventral sides look at each other, while in the marsupials they both look the same way.

Before we go into the pyramidal tract, it might be advisable to discuss briefly one more point of a more fundamental nature. It concerns the fact that the pyramidal tract cannot be the most important motor tract since it does not exist in submammalian forms, hence the center of movements from place to place must be somewhere lower in the brain. Whether it is in the reticular formation or in the midbrain is at the moment immaterial. It is certainly true that in the primates the pyramidal tract has largely taken over from the subcortical tracts of lower forms, but that is a secondary elaboration.

The number of giant pyramidal cells increases somewhat as we go from macaque to man, the only two forms for which we have numerical estimates. There are about 14,000 in the macaque and 30,000 to 40,000 in man. Since there are about half a million fibers in the pyramidal tract of the macaque and about one million fibers in that of man, the percentage of giant cells in man is only slightly greater than in the macaque (16). In both forms the vast majority of fibers comes not from giant cells but from ordinary, smaller pyramidal cells. (An old observation of mine (17), is that the size of the Betz cells increases relative to the size of the ordinary cells as we ascend the phylogenetic scale. What this means in functional terms is, however, not understood.)

The pyramidal tract arises in all likelihood from areas 6,4,1,2,3,5, and 7 (18). It is noteworthy that there is a large contribution from the parietal cortex which is almost certainly not motor in its effect and which does not exist in nonprimates. It used to be thought that the tract arose only from area 4 and that the premotor area 6 gave merely a general idea (Bewegungsentwurf (19)), while area 4 was the executive part which sent its fibers to the spinal cord. The painstaking and detailed observations of Woolsey and his collaborators (20) made it clear that this is untenable. Area 6 which has a slightly higher threshold appears to control the muscles of the back and trunk while area 4 controls primarily the muscles of the extremities, particularly of hand and foot.

In the spinal cord the tract of lower forms such as the marsupials and the rodents is in the posterior column; in higher forms, in carnivores and in primates, it is in the posterior part of the lateral column (21). The diameter of its fibers, which is an indication of the speed of conduction, gradually increases as one ascends the phylogenetic scale (22). In the opossum and the rat the fibers hardly ever become larger than 4μ. In the cat the diameter will go up as high as 8μ, and in the monkey it is about the same, while in man there are occasional fibers of a diameter of 15μ, and there is a second maximum at 11μ. The conduction time (23, 24, 25) in the rabbit is between 25 and 2 m/sec, in the cat between 70 and 10 m/sec, and in the monkey between 90 and 2 M/sec. Since we do not know enough about the endings of the fibers in the cord, we will not speculate further on the meaning of these differences.

Where does the pyramidal tract end? The immediate answer is that it goes to the spinal cord. But it also goes to numerous other points which are often overlooked when discussing the tract. There is the reticular formation, a name that comprises a variety of nuclei which are still only imperfectly understood, and which are partly motor and partly sensory in nature. Then there are the nuclei cuneatus and gracilis. Brodel (26) mentions them in the account of the nuclei gracilis and cuneatus, but does not say anything about them under the heading of the pyramidal tract. It is important to realize that these are sensory nuclei.

In the spinal cord the tract ends quite differently in different animals. When we look at the cord of a marsupial (27) we see that the pyramidal tract ends almost completely in Rexed's (28) layers III through V, spilling over only very slightly into layer VI. Among the carnivores the raccoon has some endings in layer IX around the motor cells. The cat and the dog have no fibers that go as far as layer IX where the motor cells of the anterior horn are situated.

Going directly to primates and beginning with the cord of the macaque, the tract reaches down much farther into the ventral horn and ends partly in layer IX. In the chimpanzee there is a large degeneration in IX particularly in its lateral part where the cells which send their axons to the musculature of the hand and foot are situated (29). The knowledge of the human cord is somewhat defective since very few suitable cases come to autopsy and of these only a few are performed in the appropriate fashion. There is at least one picture which confirms what one would expect from the comparative material (30).

These pictures might suggest that the pyramidal tract has no direct connections with the motor cells in lower animals, but that is not true. As Golgi preparations of the cord of the mouse show (31), the pyramidal tract is in the ventral corner of the posterior funiculus in this animal, and some of the dendrites of the big motor cells go into the neuropil formed by the pyramidal tract. The connection is weak, however, and is insufficient to bring the cell immediately to firing. There are no data on the mouse or the rat, but it is known that in the cat at least three or four impulses in the pyramidal tract are needed to fire an anterior motor horn cell, whereas in the monkey one or two impulses suffice to fire a motor cell.

The action of the pyramidal tract on lamina IV to VI must be connected with the sensory side of nervous function. It cannot be sensory proper for after all the conduction in this system goes from the center to the periphery and not the other way. It seems to exert an influence on the performance of the somesthetic system in the sense that it changes the "gating" of incoming impulses (32). By this is meant that supraspinal pathways end on internuncial cells and can, when activated, change the polarization of these internuncial cells either way, depending whether they are excitatory or inhibitory, and thus change their influence on the motor cells. This may occur on the spinal level or at the nuclei of Goll and Burdach or still higher. An example of this "gating" is what happens to the cat's sensory fields when the pyramidal tract is activated as contrasted to what the extent of the field is when the tract is quiescent (33). The receptive field of a point in the periphery enlarges considerably when pyramidal impulses are superimposed on peripheral ones.

In man, as well as in apes and the raccoon, the pyramidal tract becomes a motor tract, influencing the final common pathway. "In the higher primates the direct cortico-motoneuronal fibers make up about half of the pyramidal endings in the spinal cord. In man, the number may be even higher." (34)

It should be obvious that one should use extreme care in extrapolating results arrived at by animal experiments to man.

It also might be worthwhile to point out that one should never perceive the environment "as it actually is," but always through the changes brought about by the various "gating" mechanisms.

Seen in a wider context, it becomes fairly clear that the cortex was in the first place a sensory endstation, and that it was the main business of the pyramidal tract to "gate" the incoming information so that the right amount got through to the cortex. From this simple function there evolved gradually the motor function proper, but always in connection with sensation. Movements of the body in space and similar functions were for a long time kept at a lower level; exactly at what level is still to be investigated. In any event, the sensory primate of the cortex is to our mind, undisputed. It seems to help, now and then, to look away from the cortex itself in order to find an answer to the old question: What is the cortex all about (35)?

REFERENCES

1. Patton, H. D., and Amassian, V. E.: The pyramidal tract. Its excitation and function. In Magoun, H. W. (Ed.): *Handbook of Physiology, Section 1: Neurophysiology.* Baltimore, Williams & Wilkins, 1960, vol. II, pp. 837-862.
2. Brodmann, K.: *Vergleichende Lokalisationslehre der Grosshirnrinde.* Leipzig, J. A. Barth, 1909.
3. Cajal, S. Ramon y: *Histolgie du Systeme Nerveux de l'Homme et des Vertébrés* (translated by L. Azoulay). Paris, A. Maloine, 1911.
4. Campbell, A. W.: *Histological Studies on the Localization of Cerebral Function.* Cambridge, Harvard U Pr, 1905.
5. Economo, C. von, and Koskinas, G. N.: *Die Cytoarchitektonik der Hirnrinde des Erwachsenen Menschen.* Wien und Berlin, J. Springer, 1923.
6. Vogt, C., and Vogt, O.: Allgemeinere Ergebnisse Unserer Hirnforschung. *Z Psychol Neurol, 25:*279-401, 1919.
7. Bailey, P., and von Bonin, G.: *The Isocortex of Man.* Urbana, U of Ill Pr, 1951.
8. Mountcastle, V. B.: Afferent organization of the cortex. *Trans Am Neurol Assoc, 91:*175-180, 1966.
9. Hubel, D. H., and Wiesel, T. N.: Shape and arrangement of columns in cat's striate cortex. *J Physiol, 165:*559-568, 1963.
10. Szentagothai, J.: Architecture of the cerebral cortex. In Jaspers, H. H., Ward, A. A., and Pope, A. (Eds.): *Basic Mechanisms of the Epilepsies.* Boston, Little, 1969, pp. 13-28.
11. von Bonin, G., and Mehler, W. R.: On columnar arrangement of nerve cells in cerebral cortex. *Brain Res, 27:*1-9, 1971.
12. Katz, D.: Der aufbau der Tastwelt. *Z Psychol Physiol der Sinnesorgane Erg Bd. 11,* Leipzig, J. A. Barth, 1925.
13. Lende, R. A.: Sensory representation in the cerebral cortex of the opossum. *J Comp Neurol, 121:*395-404, 1963.
14. Lende, R. A.: Motor representation in the cerebral cortex of the opossum. *J Comp Neurol, 121:*405-416, 1963.
15. Penfield W., and Rasmussen, T.: *The Cerebral Cortex of Man.* New York, Macmillan, 1950.
16. Lassek, A. M.: *The Pyramidal Tract, Its Status in Medicine.* Springfield, Thomas, 1954.

17. von Bonin, G.: Studies of the cells in the cerebral cortex. II. The motor area in man, cebus, and cat. *J Comp Neurol, 69*:381-390, 1938.
18. Foerster, O.: Motorische felder u Bahnen. In Foerster, O. and Bumke, D. (Eds.): *Handbook of Physiology.* Baltimore, Williams & Wilkins, 1933, vol. VI.
19. Liepmann, H.: *Drei Aufsatze aus dem Apraxiegebiet.* Berlin, S. Karger, 1908.
20. Woolsey, C. N., et al.: Pattern of localization in precentral and supplementary motor areas and their relation to the concept of a premotor area. *Assoc Res Nerv Ment Dis, 30*:238-264, 1952.
21. Fuse, G.: Vergleichend Anatomische Beobachtungen am Hirnstamm der Saeugetiere. *Arb Anat Inst, der K Japan, Univ zu Sendai, 12*:47-82, 1926.
22. Woolsey, C. N., and Chang, H. T.: Activation of the cerebral cortex by antidromic volleys in the pyramidal tract. *Assoc Res Nerv Ment Dis, 27*:146-161, 1948.
23. Biedenbach, M. A., and Towe, A. L.: Fiberspectrum and functional properties of pyramidal tract neurons in the American opossum. *J Comp Neurol, 140*:421-429, 1970.
24. Haeggquist, G.: Analyse der Faserverteilung in einem Ruckenmarksquerschnitt (Th. 3). *Z Mikrosk Anat Forsch, 29*:1-34, 1936.
25. Towe, A. L.: Relative number of pyramidal tract neurons in mammals of different size. *Brain Behav Evol, 7*:1-17, 1973.
26. Brodal, A.: *Neurological Anatomy in Relation to Clinical Medicine.* Oxford, Clarendon, 1948.
27. Martin, G. F., Megirian, D., and Roebuck, A.: The corticospinal tract of the marsupial phalanger. *J Comp Neurol, 139*:245-255, 1970.
28. Rexed, B.: The cytoarchitectonic organization of the spinal cord in the cat. *J Comp Neurol, 96*:415-495, 1952.
29. Petras, J. M.: Some efferent connections of the motor and somatosensory cortex of simian primates and felines, canid and procyonid carnivores. *Ann NY Acad Sci, 167*:469-505, 1969.
30. Schoen, J. H. R.: Comparative aspects of the descending fibre system. In Eccles, J. C., and Schade, P.: *Organization of the Spinal Cord.* Amsterdam, Elsevier, 1964, vol. II, pp. 203-222.
31. Valverde, F.: The pyramidal tract in rodents. *Z Zellforsch Mikrosk Anat, 71*:297-363, 1966.
32. Granit, R., and Burke, R. E.: The control of movement and posture. *Brain Res, 53*:1-28, 1973.
33. Wall, P. D.: The sensory systems. In Rosenblith, W. (Ed.): *Symposium on Sensory Communication.* New York, Wiley, 1961, pp. 475-495.
34. Adkins, R. J., Morse, J. R., and Towe, A. L.: Control of somato sensory input by cerebral cortex. *Science, 153*:1020-1022, 1966.
35. Gooddy, W., and Reinhold, M.: The function of the cerebral cortex. *Brain, 77*:416-426, 1954.

Chapter 5

BRAIN WAVE EVOKED POTENTIALS, THE CLASSIFICATION OF CHILDREN WITH MINIMAL BRAIN DYSFUNCTION, AND PREDICTION OF RESPONSE TO STIMULANT MEDICATION

Enoch Callaway

THE diagnosis of minimal brain dysfunction (or MBD) seems to be used when things are not going as well for a child as they should. That is to say when gross social stresses, obvious physical disease, bizarre thought disorders, and definite mental retardation are not apparent, then we expect a child to adapt to family, friends, and schoolwork within certain limits. Given no gross physical or social pathology, the brain is the organ responsible for successful adaptation, and in such unsuccessful children we can legitimately make the diagnosis of minimal brain dysfunction. Such circular thinking helps hide ignorance, and that may be useful in the clinic. When we have time to step back from our practices, however, we would like something more scientific — that is to say we would like diagnoses that address real causes, suggest specific remedies, and are not just rephrased descriptions of what the patient already knows.

Now there are two other ways of classifying MBD — one *a priori* and one *a posteriori*. *A priori*, they fall into three clumps — hyperactive, normoactive, and hypoactive. *A posteriori*, they can be classified according to whether stimulant medications (such as amphetamine or methylphenidate) have helped. Here we will be

From the Langley Porter Neuropsychiatric Institute and the Department of Psychiatry, University of California, San Francisco Medical Center. This research was supported by NICHD grant HD 03107 and NIMH grant MH 22149.

discussing children whose most prominent symptom was hyperactivity.

Unfortunately, as Barbara Fish (1) has pointed out, activity is a poor predictor of response to stimulants. Both over- and underactive children may be helped. With the exception of the observation that children with severe thought disorders do poorly on stimulants, she has little more than a kind of athletic empiricism to offer the clinician.

There are, however, some indications that although clinical observation does not distinguish easily in advance between children whom stimulants will help and those whom stimulants will not help, the brain wave may give better clues.

The best and most simple example is found in a study just reported by Satterfield (2). The worse the EEG, the better the response of hyperkinetic children to a stimulant. It has long been recognized that even patients with gross neurological disorders may benefit from stimulants, but there is a persistent tendency to view stimulants as "psychoactive" drugs to be used to modify the psyche and not to be used if the brain (soma) is obviously involved. Satterfield shows that when the brain dysfunction is of the sort to be reflected in the EEG, then that dysfunction is more amenable to pharmacologic modification by stimulants.

The finding is clinically useful, but it also makes appealingly good sense. Overt behavioral pathology represents the interaction between external stress and the individuals' own weaknesses. The more the defect is in an individual (and reciprocally the less in his environment), the more a medication directed to the individual should be expected to help with the disordered behavior.

The EEG is a gross reflection of a potpourri of activity going on in the brain all at the same time. By using various computer-based techniques, more specific aspects of the brain electrical activity can be separated. Among these newer techniques, the best known involves averaging evoked potentials.

To study evoked potentials, the trick is to get the brain to do the same thing repeatedly at known times. Samples of electrical activity timed as accurately as possible to these specific brain activities are taken by the computer and averaged so that the random background activity cancels out and the repeated electrical concomitant of the repeated brain activity is summed and so made to stand out.

These averaged evoked potentials (or AEP) can be obtained by presenting repeated stimulus such as a tone or light flashes. The AEP depends, of course, in part on the evoking stimulus, but more important, it also depends very much on the subject's psychological attitude to the evoking stimulus. In general, the more interested in the stimulus the subject is, the larger is the AEP, particularly the late components. If this interest is stable and sustained, the variability of the evoked potentials also declines.

The next step is almost too obvious. The syndrome of MBD is really a syndrome of disattention. In the AEP we have a measure of attention that is made at the level of the brain and prior to voluntary skeletal motor responses. One should be able to use AEP to study MBD.

Satterfield has already made use of the AEP in studying the hyperkinetic child. He had his children watching movies of Bugs Bunny and Roadrunner while tones were sounding. The more the child attended to the movies, the smaller the evoked potentials. Also, younger (and perhaps more immature) children show smaller evoked potentials. The hyperkinetic children had smaller AEPs than age matched controls, and Satterfield interpreted this as relative immaturity of the hyperkinetic children, but it could also have indicated that the child who is easily distracted in class may show fantastic concentration when hypnotized by the "one-eyed baby-sitter." Satterfield also examined his children after treatment with stimulants and noted that the small AEPs had become even smaller in the children who had had good responses. Remember, however, that this was after chronic treatment and not in response to an acute dose.

Our strategy was somewhat different from Satterfield's. Let us suppose that there may be a variety of disattentions. A number of different defects may prevent the effective direction of attention. The resulting disattention may then in turn result in under or over activity depending on various other factors, such as the nature of the child and the responses of his environment. Suppose also that only certain forms of disattention are responsive to stimulant medication. We thus should look for some measures of attention that stimulants affect and that also differentiate between MBD children who respond to stimulants and those who do not.

Let's call this imaginary measure of disattention "X." Ideally a stimulant should reduce "X." MBD children who are helped by stimulants should be higher on "X" than stimulant-treatment failures or normal children, and thus a test dose of a stimulant should normalize "X" in responsive children. We then set off on a series of pilot studies in search of measure "X."

There are an almost infinite number of ways one can record the EEG, and almost as many different ways one can measure the resulting AEPs. We began with a broad shotgun type of approach, and of course found several candidates; but when one surveys a large number of possibilities, some are bound to look good by chance alone. We use a series of pilot studies, so as to repeat measures that looked good in earlier studies, discard failures, and try new ideas. We are now in the third pass, and I will spend most of my remaining time on one of the measures that held up in all three studies. However, I will also describe some of the other new, but as yet not so well tried candidates.

The measure of interest is called the normalized standard deviation, or NSD. The important facts are (1) that NSD goes up the more the individual evoked potential varies from stimulus to stimulus; (2) that NSD goes down the larger the amplitude of the averaged evoked potential. Thus it taps the two aspects of evoked potential that attention generally influences. Since attention decreases variability and increases amplitudes of EP, it should lower NSD.

Our first study involved hyperkinetic MBD children who had responded to amphetamines, children who had failed to respond on a trial of amphetamines and some controls. All were males quite close to age nine. We presented intermixed tones and flashes under three conditions. First, there was no assigned task; we call that nonattending. Then the children were asked to press a key when they heard occasional tones of a different pitch. That we call auditory attending. Finally, they were asked to respond to slightly dimmer flashes, and that we call visual attending. Normal children and MBD children who had not responded favorably to amphetamines did not differ on the NSD scores, so we pooled them to produce the measures shown in Table 5-1. In passing it is worth noting that this similarity in AEPs of normals and MBD-amphetamine nonresponders has been noted by other investigators.

TABLE 5-I

VISUAL AEP NORMALIZED STANDARD DEVIATION

PILOT STUDY

		Auditory	*visual*
	Nonattending	*Attending*	*Attending*
Responders	960	959	959
Nonresponders & Controls	925	942	934

Table 5-1 shows NSD for visual AEPs. By analysis of variance, the subjects times attention interaction was significant at p .05. Note that responders have high NSD scores and show very little change under the different conditions of attention. Note also for the normals and nonresponders the NSD to the flashes is somewhat larger with visual attention late in the session than during the initial nonattending condition. It seems that the novelty caused the children to attend more than the simple task given last in a series of three tiring sittings.

The MBD children were also tested in counterbalanced order with and without amphetamines (normal children were, of course, not given drugs). Amphetamine reduced NSD significantly. Thus the criteria for measure "X" were met. Amphetamines did not, however, increase the effects of attention.

Next we tried to use AEP measures to predict clinical response to amphetamines. Children who were due for a clinical trial of stimulant medication were brought to the laboratory in the morning. A visual attending run was done, followed by a nonattending run. Then at lunchtime 5 mg of amphetamine was given and the child was tested again.

The children then were put on amphetamines and ratings from teachers and parents were collected. The results were a disaster as far as research was concerned. The correlations between the improvement ratings by teachers, parents, and the pediatrician were low. We found, for example, that one teacher rated the child before giving drug, but had the volunteer teachers aide do the second ratings, "because she (the aide) as feeling left out." Furthermore, the AEP results did not show that amphetamines had improved attention much in any child; as though the increase in attention produced by the amphetamine and the decreased attention produced by doing two test settings in the same day just about cancelled out.

The clinical response was then further evaluated by visits from the psychologist and phone calls by the pediatrician. The following summer the children returned to the laboratory for three tests — a pretest and two drug tests — one with amphetamine and one with placebo. Half had amphetamines before placebo and half placebo before amphetamine. All tests were in the morning and at least three days elapsed between test days.

The complex results are shown in Figure 5-1. On the left we see the insignificant morning- afternoon study, on the right we see the results from the summer study. In this later (summer) study the analysis of variance was significant for attention, for drugs, and for drugs by attention, so we do have some positive results. Note, first, that almost all the NSD values are high. Only one of these unselected MBD children have values in the low range of the normals and of the selected nonresponders. Note that in general attention/first sitting values are lower than nonattending second sitting values. This was always the case in the very first (AM) sitting and in the summer drug sessions. It looks as though novelty and amphetamines have similar effects. Clinically the children also appear to be much more tractable the first time in the lab, only to show their hyperactivity fully after they become familiar with the surroundings. We will come to the four dark lines labeled A and B later.

If we compare placebo and amphetamine sessions during the summer study (when the children were familiar with the

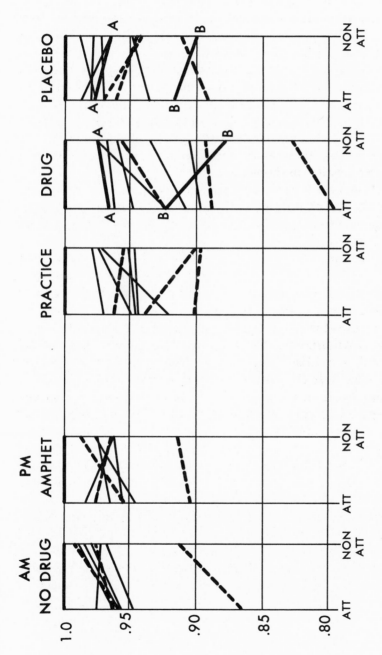

Figure 5-1. NSD values for visual AEPs recorded under attending and nonattending conditions. Dotted lines indicate children with good clinical responses to amphetamines. Dark lines are new (Ritalin) subjects.

laboratory) we see amphetamine regularly reduces the NSD and increases the effects of attention. The three best responders also show two things in common. They do not have extremely high NSD values and do show good amphetamine effects (i.e. lowering of NSD and increase of attention effects).

We now have a somewhat more elaborate rule. Response to amphetamine as measured by NSD is greater in MBD children who will respond to amphetamine clinically. But very high NSD is a poor sign. This latter point is not as surprising as it sounds. It has previously been found that NSD high in schizophrenia adults and schizophrenic-like thought disorders is one of the poor prognostic signs Fish noted (3).

We have a set of rules, but we have altered them to fit each study. Second, we had to use a subjective and very "un-blind" method to determine whether or not the child was helped by amphetamines.

The third study is currently underway so the last chapter is not written yet. The design is essentially the same as the summer session for the second group of children that has just been discussed. The recording techniques are somewhat improved, and the clinical ratings vastly improved. We have been forced to change to Ritalin® for political reasons. We now use a "target symptom" checklist designed for each child, and when the pediatrician feels the dose is optimal we do a five-day double-blind parent and teacher rating with two days placebo and three days drug. Thus we can estimate the variance as well as the level of ratings both on and off drugs.

So far we have run eighteen new children, but final response to medication has been rated in only a few. By good luck, however, the first two children included one who had clear-cut good response to Ritalin, with a very questionable therapeutic response who, by our "target symptom blind-trial" procedure, qualified as a nonresponder.

The dark lines in Figure 5-1 show the visual NSD measures made on the potentials evoked by the flashes when the two Ritalin subjects were watching for dim flashes (attending) and when they had no special task other than to look at the lights (nonattending). Note that both children showed a reversed affect of attending with placebo. NSD was higher attending than nonattending. With Ritalin, however, one child is normalized and shows a reduced NSD during attention. Neither have extremely high NSD values, so by our rule the child (A) with the positive AEP response to Ritalin before treatment should have been the one to show a favorable clinical response, and so it was.

The odds of hitting two out of two by chance are .25, hardly an acceptable p value, but we will soon have sixteen more cases and the odds (based on the two preceding studies) are pretty fair that this will hold up.

The overall picture can be seen by examining the results obtained from subject A, the Ritalin responder. Figure 5-2 shows auditory AEP on the left and visual on the right. Recordings are made from three electrode positions: left central (C3), right central (C4), and vertex (Cz) and referred to as linked ears, but only the vertex AEPs are shown. There are three conditions: attending, nonattending and self-stimulating. This last is obtained by having the child press a switch to produce the tone, and of course yields only an auditory AEP.

Note first that visual AEP amplitude is highest in nonattending with placebo, but slightly higher in attention with Ritalin. Ritalin makes the earlier component of the self-stimulated AEP smaller and makes the later component larger. This appears to be the more normal pattern.

Ritalin did not normalize the AEPs of the nonresponder (B), and this is shown in Figure 5-3.

In conclusion, we begin to see the glimmering of a coherent picture. If a child has AEP abnormalities that are corrected by a challenge dose of medication, we then predict that child will be benefited by a clinical trial. The particular AEP measures that are used appear to be measures that are sensitive to attention; this makes sense if we consider that minimal brain disorder is primarily a disorder of attention.

What about the practical utility of such a test — assuming of course that the results continue to support our current view of things. We need three morning's time from the child, a parent, and a technician, plus about $250,000 worth of equipment. This is hardly something for the neighborhood pediatrician. As for

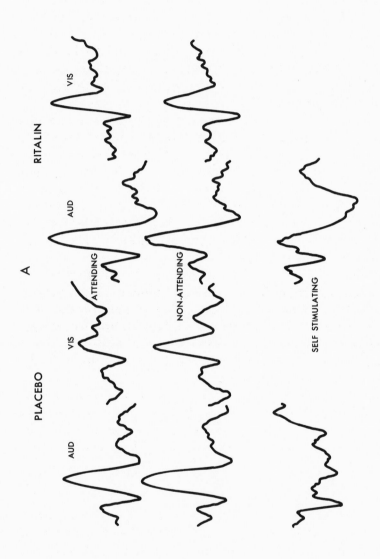

Figure 5-2. Subject A — good clinical response to Ritalin.

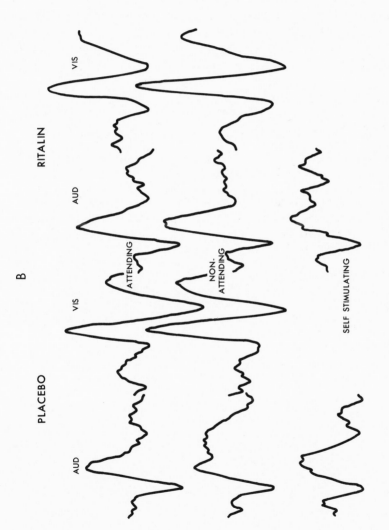

Figure 5-3. Subject B — poor clinical response to Ritalin.

time, once we are sure we have a real finding, we can perhaps streamline things. As for equipment, we are building a unit now that is far superior to our present arrangement which will cost under $15,000. The new central computer costs about $8,000; and within a few years with parts currently available, but as yet not packaged for the small user, such a unit could be put together for under $4,000. Thus, we feel that as preliminary as this work is, it is at a stage where the clinician might well find it of interest. At least I hope so.

REFERENCES

1. Fish, B.: The "one child, one drug" myth of stimulants in hyperkinesis. *Arch Gen Psychiatry, 25*:193, 1971.
2. Satterfield, J. H.: EEG issues in children with minimal brain dysfunction. *Seminars in Psychiatry, 5*:35, 1973.
3. Jones, R. T., and Callaway, E.: Auditory evoked responses in schizophrenia — a reassessment. *Biol Psychiatry, 2*:291, 1970.
4. Cassaway, E., and Halliday, R. A.: Evoked potential variability: Effects of age, amplitude and methods of measurement. *Electroencephalogr Clin Neurophysiol, 34*:125, 1973.

Chapter 6

ABNORMAL SEROTONERGIC MECHANISMS OF SLEEP REGULATION IN ALCOHOLISM

VINCENT P. ZARCONE, JR.

THERE are many clinical observations which lead one to hypothesize a connection between disordered sleep and alcoholism. Anyone who has had personal experience with acute ethanol intoxication knows that sleep may be disturbed after social drinking. Even four or five drinks spread over two hours can result in awakening from sleep often in the middle of the night with a dry mouth, headache, fast heart and respiration rate, and the feeling that things are going to be worse the next morning. Sleep continues to be disturbed after this first awakening and there may be more intense dreaming approaching the quality of a delirium.

In more pathologic drinking, there is more profound sleep disturbance. The alcoholic, and this includes most of the men in the studies that we have done, report that at the beginning of a heavy drinking period the alcohol ingestion leads to a feeling of heightened awareness of the surroundings, mild euphoria, an increase in activity; these changes may be associated with an improvement in sleep. But, after one or two days of heavy drinking, sleep begins to get more and more disturbed. It becomes increasingly fragmented so that if the alcoholic is not a complete insomniac, he begins to sleep in brief two- or three-hour periods around the clock; as the heavy drinking period lengthens, he begins to drink in order to get some sleep and some relief from the sickness that he feels accumulating.

During the alcoholic withdrawal syndromes, sleep is profoundly disturbed. There is often insomnia, the fragmentation of sleep continues, and the patient feels very frightened by the heightened state of excitability and the lack of sleep. The acute ethanol withdrawal syndrome is often dramatically reversed at the time of the first long, uninterrupted sleep (this sleep has come to be called a *critical sleep*). In the chronic alcoholic withdrawal syndrome, which goes on for at least six weeks and may continue longer, the alcoholic feels hyperexcitable. He still notes that he has a sleep disturbance which contributes to his craving for alcohol. He believes that if he drinks a little bit, it will help him sleep at night.

These kinds of clinical observations have motivated us at Stanford University to undertake a systematic investigation of the relationship between sleep disordering and alcoholism. The descriptions of our studies will be divided into five parts. The first part will involve a brief review of human sleep physiology. The second part will be devoted to a discussion of the underlying neural mechanisms in the brain stem which we believe to be important in regulating sleep. The third part of the discussion will review the effects of ethanol ingestion on sleep in human subjects. The fourth part will give a more detailed look at one of the studies which we have done at Stanford, namely the studies of the effect of serotonin precursor loading on the sleep of alcoholics during chronic withdrawal syndrome. The final part of the discussion will be a look at some of the limitations of the interpretations that we make of our data.

There are three states of vigilance in humans: nonrapid eye movement sleep (non-REM), REM, and waking (1). Non-REM sleep is divided into stages 1 through 4 and are characterized by alpha blocking, K-complex, and spindles and delta waves. Rapid eye movement sleep is characterized by tonic inhibition of the peripheral musculature, tonic activation of the EEG, and various phasic events. The phasic events of REM sleep include the rapid eye movements, which gives the stage its name; contractions of the middle ear muscles; autonomic variability, that is variability of the heart rate and respiration rate; contractions of the external laryngeal muscles; and the psychologic state of vivid perceptual-like or quality hallucinations which are called *dreaming*. If a human subject is awakened from rapid eye movement periods, he reports dreaming or dream-like experience about 80 to 95 per cent of the time. When awakened from non-REM sleep, he reports mentation of a more abstract or more cognitive quality, about 70 per cent of the time. Deprivation of state REM results in a compensatory increase during subsequent ad lib sleep; that is, a REM rebound. Deprivation of stage 4 also results in a rebound of stage 4. In the last three years, we have come to view these cycles of non-REM and REM sleep occurring throughout the night as a collection of processes which have some overlap. The fact is that phasic events which ordinarily occur in rapid eye movement sleep also occur in non-REM sleep in twenty or thirty seconds preceding rapid eye movement sleep periods, and they can be further dissociated from rapid eye movement sleep into non-REM sleep by giving various drugs. Therefore, the phasic events of REM sleep have a separate mechanism from that which controls the tonic events of REM sleep, and the tonic and phasic events can be dissociated from each other.

There is a ninety-minute cycle of non-REM, REM sleep during the night. It is important to emphasize that most of the stage 3 and 4 sleep or delta sleep occurs in the first half of the night and most of the REM sleep occurs in the second half of the night. The delta sleep in the first half of the night is associated with the secretion of human growth hormone (2) and the REM sleep occurring in the second half of the night is associated with the secretion of corticosteroid hormone (3). There is also some evidence to indicate that prolactin secretion is a function of sleep, at least during puberty.

Sleep cycles are obviously interrelated with other biologic rhythms of a circadian sort. During this discussion, we will be ignoring this interaction between the various circadian rhythms of the organism and the ultradian, or ninety-minute REM, non-REM cycle. We will also be ignoring the fact that the prior amount of wakefulness determines to some extent the sleep staging throughout the night. We feel that we can ignore these major sources of variance at some risk, but we have taken the risk; otherwise it wouldn't be possible to do our studies. We do try to control for circadian effects by adhering to a rigid sleep period for our subjects and, of course, we control as well as we can for the amount of prior wakefulness by doing our studies in a hospital setting where we can observe the patients and make sure that they do not nap during the daytime. We also control for a third major source of variability in the sleep cycle by limiting the amount of external stimulation. All of our studies are done in sound and light attenuated rooms (1).

Michel Jouvet's review in the *Review of Physiology* (5) describes the brain stem neuronal systems which are important in sleep regulation. Acetylcholine and short chain fatty acid systems which may be involved in sleep regulation are not described in this review. The monoamine hypothesis of sleep regulation began to be formed in 1964 with the observation of reserpine's effect on sleep. Reserpine, in a dose of 5 mg per kilo, causes a profound disruption of sleep regulation and behavior. It produces an insomnia which can be reversed by giving various drugs: L-Dopa reverses the disturbance in REM sleep and L-5HTP reverses the disturbance in slow wave sleep or non-REM sleep. This observation, of course, provoked a good deal of subsequent work on the monoamine systems in the brain stem whose function was as yet unknown. The work proceeded, using two strategies in which sleep and sleep staging were the dependent variables. The first strategy involves surgical lesioning of various parts of the brain stem and the second strategy involves pharmacologic lesions. The surgical lesion and pharmacologic studies have been greatly aided by the coincident development of histo-fluoresence techniques for determining the effects of lesions and pharmacologic intervention on monoaminergic cell bodies, axones and terminals in the brain. The brain stem neuronal systems which regulate sleep project both rostrally throughout the brain and caudally into the spinal cord.

The nigro striatal system seems to be involved in the regulation of behavior wakefulness. The studies done to date involve lesions in the substantia nigra area which projects into the rest of the extra-pyramidal system. Lesions in the substantia nigra result in a cat which has normal EEG wake-sleep cycles but is behaviorally depressed, almost comatose.

The locus coeruleus, and sub-coeruleus are involved in the regulation of both REM phasic events and tonic inhibition of the peripheral musculature. There is some controversy as to just what the connections and inhibitions and facilitations in this area are. However, it appears that the rostral part of the locus coeruleus is involved in the maintenance of a normal waking EEG dysynchrony. The middle part of the locus coeruleus and sub-coeruleus area is involved in the generation of REM phasic events, and the caudal portion is involved in the inhibition of peripheral musculature at the anterior horn cell level which produces the profound muscle inhibition of rapid eye movement sleep.

The serotonergic midline raphe neurons extend through the pontine reticular formation in the midline and project both caudally and rostrally, all the way to the cortex. Lesions of this area produce an insomnia which is reversible by administration of 5-hydroxytryptophan (5HTP). Pharmacologic lesions of this area, that is with parachlorophenylalanine which blocks the synthesis of serotonin at the tryptophan hydroxylase step, are also reversible with administration of 5 HTP. There is a relationship between the extent of the surgical lesion and the amount of 5HTP necessary to reverse the disturbance in slow wave sleep. Similarly, there is a direct relationship between the size of the raphe lesions and the decrease of histo-fluorescense following the lesion and the subsequent slow wave sleep decrease. Finally, it is important to realize that this midline raphe system is also involved in the regulation of rapid eye movement sleep. If there is a total surgical lesion or pharmacologic lesion of this system, there is no rapid eye movement sleep. It seems necessary that slow wave sleep be present at least 15 per cent of a 24-hour period in order for some rapid eye movement sleep to occur. This had led Jouvet to hypothesize that the turnover of serotonin through the oxidated step to 5-hydroxyindoleacetic acid is important in intiating REM phasic event activity. Activity in the serotonergic system may be necessary in order for rapid eye movement sleep to continue at a level of intensity such that the organism is not aroused. These neurons can be viewed as partially inhibitory to the locus coeruleus which initiate or are the executive mechanism for rapid eye movement sleep and particularly REM phasic events. This serotonergic system is important, not only during rapid eye movement sleep, but also during waking. When PCPA is given, it not only produces an insomnia, but also produces rather profound effects on behavior with an increase in aggressiveness and sexuality. We hypothesize that a release of REM phasic event activity or a failure of serotonergic raphe inhibition underlies these behaviors.

It is also important to note that tricyclic antidepressants and MAO inhibitors have an effect on these systems. Both drugs produce a decrease of REM sleep without affecting slow wave sleep. The MAO inhibitor blocks the step from serotonin to the oxidated metabolites, and this fact of the differential effect of MAO inhibitors on REM and non-REM sleep caused Jouvet to hypothesize that the 5HT metabolites were important in the initiation of rapid eye movement sleep.

The acute effects of ethanol on normal subjects can be summarized easily (6). Alcohol, like many other drugs — including heroin, tricyclic antidepressants, MAO inhibitors, barbiturates, amphetamines, and marijuana — is a REM suppressant. It is a rather potent REM suppressant and tolerance to the REM suppressing effects of ethanol develop over a period of two to three nights. If about two to three ounces of ethanol is given to a normal subject, he will show an increase in heart rate, an increase in respiration rate, an increase of fast activity in the EEG, a decrease in REM time and some increase in slow wave sleep. During a withdrawal period there is REM rebound.

The effects of ethanol in alcoholics is essentially the same, except that during the acute withdrawal stage, that is from day 1 through days 6 through 10 of withdrawal, the REM rebound can be quite significantly increased, compared to what is seen in normal subjects. Normal subjects can rebound in the second half of the night from a small dose of ethanol before bedtime, but the alcoholic in a heavy drinking period seems to accumulate a tremendous REM pressure which is manifested by very high REM times during withdrawal and very intense rapid eye movement sleep periods. These observations were made by Greenberg and Pearlman (7) and Gross, et al. (8). Up to 100 per cent of sleep time was rapid eye movement sleep, and this alternated with hallucinations. This leads us to assume that during withdrawal there is a neuronal supersensitivity state in which neurons which initiate REM phasic events are overactive, or that there is a failure of inhibition by a serotonergic system or both. This allows for a kind of free-running REM phasic event system during acute withdrawal.

The chronic ethanol withdrawal syndrome, i.e. beginning some time around the sixth withdrawal day and lasting varying periods of time, may or may not be reversible. We hypothesize that in alcoholism there is a continuum of changes from neurotransmitter depletion to receptor sensitivity changes to neuronal protein synthesis defects to structural damage.

In the chronic withdrawal syndrome, REM sleep remains fragmented. There is an abnormality of stage 2 K-complex formation, and there is a decrease in delta sleep. In some of our chronic alcoholics we have noticed a marked decrease in delta sleep which has persisted for as long as three months following the last heavy drinking period. Allen, et al. (9) has noted similar findings. We feel that there are some alcoholics who manifest an irreversible brain syndrome in that they have a markedly disturbed sleep with a decrease or absence of delta sleep and

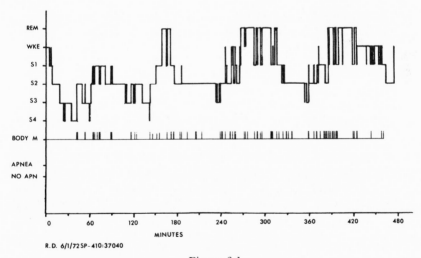

R.D. 6/1/72 SP-410:37040

Figure 6-1.

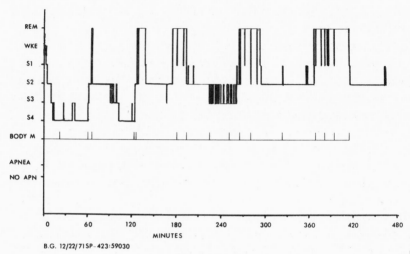

B.G. 12/22/71SP-423:59030

Figure 6-2.

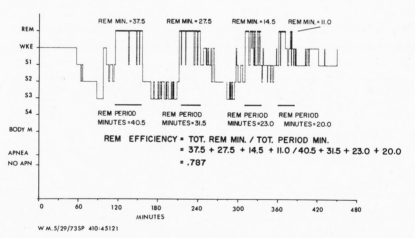

W M. 5/29/73SP 410:45121

Figure 6-3.

fragmentation of REM periods. Figures 6-1 and 6-2 compare the normal staging of sleep in an alcoholic who is almost completely recovered from his last heavy drinking period and one who is not. There is fragmentation and interruption of sleep in the latter subject particularly in REM periods, and there is a marked decrease in delta sleep.

Figure 6-3 defines REM efficiency. This parameter is important in understanding the major effects on the sleep of alcoholics following precursor loading. The definition of REM efficiency involves the fact that REM periods can continue uninterrupted or they can be frequently interrupted. If they are frequently interrupted, we speak of this as fragmentation; we guess that this is an abnormality that is peculiar to the disturbance in the serotonergic system which regulates rapid eye movement sleep as well as slow wave sleep.

We hypothesize that in an abnormal system such as in chronic alcohol withdrawal syndromes, 5HTP might improve sleep. To test the effectiveness of 5HTP during ethanol withdrawal, we compared the administration of 5HTP 300 mg and inactive placebo in a group of twelve abstinent alcoholics (10). The subjects' ages ranged from twenty-five to fifty-two years (mean=40.7 years). Most of the subjects had been drinking for more than five years. The range in drinking history was from three to thirty-four years (mean= 14.3 years). All had been dry for twenty-three to 133 days (means=50.1 days) prior to the study. Urine samples of eight subjects were collected following selected drug and placebo nights to insure that the 5HTP was actually absorbed and metabolized by the body through the oxidating pathway to 5HIAA. In each subject, there was a marked increase in excretion of 5HIAA following drug nights which resulted in a highly significant difference (p=.004, Binomial Tests) between placebo and drug levels.

The design of the present study was relatively simple. Each subject slept in a sound-attenuated, light-attenuated, temperature-controlled room for fourteen consecutive nights. All subjects maintained a total dark time in bed of eight hours (from 10:30 PM to 6:30 AM). The first night of the study was used to accommodate the subjects to the laboratory surroundings. Nights

2 through 6 were baseline nights, nights 7 through 11 were drug nights, and nights 11 through 14 were recovery nights.

Each night, subjects received one capsule at 7:30 PM and two capsules at 9:00 PM. On drug nights the capsules contained 100 mg of L-5HTP; on placebo nights the capsules contained lactose. Throughout the study the subjects were given bedtime and morning questionnaires to assess the quality of sleep and side effects. There were no significant subjective effects from drug administration. One subject reported abdominal pain on one placebo and one drug night. The subjects were unaware of which nights were placebo and which were drug.

The sleep records were scored in thirty-second epochs according to the criterion of the Standard Sleep Scoring Manual. The scoring was done by persons who were unaware of any experimental manipulations.

TABLE 6-I

GRAND MEAN, STANDARD DEVIATIONS AND SIGNIFICANCE LEVELS
OF SLEEP VARIABLE DATA COLLECTED FROM ALL SUBJECTS.

Sleep Variable	CONDITION			Signi-ficance Levels
	Baseline (B) (mean ± S.D.)	Drug (D) (mean ± S.D.)	Recovery (R) (mean ± S.D.)	
Sleep Latency (min.)	22.7 ± 12.7	23.8 ± 13.2	27.6 ± 17.1	N.S.
Wake Time After Sleep Onset (min.)	38.6 ± 19.4	34.4 ± 16.5	39.7 ± 15.6	N.S.
% Stage 1	17.8 ± 4.2	14.3 ± 3.8	14.4 ± 3.8	B D**
				B R*
% Stage 2	45.7 ± 5.1	48.4 ± 5.3	48.5 ± 3.8	D B*
% Stage 3	9.0 ± 3.4	10.0 ± 2.9	10.3 ± 2.9	N.S.
% Stage 4	5.2 ± 1.8	3.3 ± 2.0	2.9 ± 1.6	N.S.
% Stage REM	22.3 ± 4.1	22.7 ± 4.0	22.7 ± 5.4	N.S.
REM Efficiency	.766 ± .08	.800 ± .08	.773 ± .07	D R*

*P ≥ .01
**p ≥ .05, matched sample T-tests, 2-tailed.

Table 6-I shows the tabulated sleep variables in our group of subjects. It is noted that drug effects were predominant in stages 1 and 2 and in REM efficiency.

REM efficiency (RE) reflects the degree of REM period fragmentation. A lower RE corresponds to greater REM period fragmentation. RE was found to improve with 5HTP administration over the baseline placebo condition in nine of the twelve subjects. It is interesting to note that the three subjects who showed no improvement in RE with 5HTP all had basal RE values of greater than .900, while those who showed improvement had RE values of less than .900. The values are shown in Table 6-II.

TABLE 6-II

MEAN REM EFFICIENCIES (RE) OF SUBJECTS

Subject	Group 1 Conditions			Subject	Group 2 Conditions		
	Baseline	Drug	Recovery		Baseline	Drug	Recovery
A	.676	.795	.721	J	.944	.864	.850
B	.764	.784	.747	K	.972	.955	.912
C	.564	.611	.572	L	.950	.905	.951
D	.669	.704	.662				
E	.850	.867	.790				
F	.699	.839	.807				
G	.771	.843	.832				
H	.684	.728	.738				
I	.627	.708	.699				

*The subjects are divided into two groups according to whether REM efficiency increased with 5 HTP administration. Two-tailed, matched sample T-tests were employed within the first group. Drug RE was significantly greater than baseline (p .01) or recovery (p .05) values.

Moreover, a significant Spearman RHO correlation of $r_s = .699$ (p$\leqslant$.05) revealed that those who had the lowest REM efficiencies during baseline had the greatest increase in REM efficiency during the drug period. Hence, the degree of improvement on 5HT was directly related to the degree of impairment on baseline nights.

Similarly, while REM percentage did not significantly improve between conditions, a high inverse correlation ($r_s = .757$; p$\leqslant$.01) existed between REM percentage during baseline and increase in that variable with drug administration. No such increase was found in stage 3. These relationships are summarized in Table 6-III.

TABLE 6-III

SPEARMAN RHO CORRELATIONS

-.699	(p ⩽ .05)	REM Efficiency correlated between baseline values and increases with drug.
-.757	(p ⩽ .01)	REM percentage correlated between baseline and increases with drug.
.084	(N.S.)	Stage 3 percentage correlated between baseline values and increases with drug.
-.886	(p ⩽ .05)	REM efficiency correlated between baseline values and drinking history (total number of past drinking days) for *S*s dry for 31 days or less.
-.143	(N.S.)	Same — for *S*s dry longer than 31 days.

It occurred to us that 5HTP may be more effective when given during early ethanol withdrawal. To clarify this, we divided subjects into two groups; (1) those who had been dry for thirty-one days or less and (2) those who had been withdrawn for a longer period. We then correlated drinking history (total number of past drinking days) with basal REM times. A significant correlation was found with subjects who were dry for thirty-one days or less, but little correlation with subjects withdrawn for a longer period. Hence, we postulate that the greater the drinking history, the more effect 5HTP will have in increasing REM efficiency during early withdrawal.

Finally, let us give some consideration to the limitations of interpretation of these data and also of our approach in this area. One limitation has to do with the fact that 5HTP loading may not result in a physiologic distribution of usable serotonin at axonal terminals. In fact, 5HTP when given to normal organisms is decarboxylated extra-neuronally in a very unphysiologic way (11). However, Agijanian (12) has pointed out that raphe cell fluorescense is not appreciably increased by the systemic administration of 5HTP except in the presence of monoamine oxidase inhibitors, that is, in an abnormal system. In this regard, it is interesting to note that Williams and Salamy (13) have suggested that long-term alcohol effects may resemble MAOI effects. Similar results have been found by several investigators (14, 15, 16, 17, 18, 19) in that 5HTP in fact does reverse the PCPA produced abnormalities in cat sleep. 5HTP also corrects PCPA induced abnormalities in man, that is in patients given PCPA for carcinoid syndrome (20).

We should further note that it is unlikely that ethanol produces a single abnormality in sleep regulating systems. We noted that there is little correlation between stage 3 increases with 5HTP and baseline values of stage 3, and this bothers us somewhat. It may perhaps be explained by the fact that some patients have irreversible changes in slow wave sleep regulation that only a percentage of patients can show an increase in delta sleep. We are continuing to look for sub-groups of alcoholics on the assumption that some alcoholics with decreased delta sleep will be able to show an increase with 5HTP.

Another obvious limitation on interpretation of this work is the fact that we have not done a dose response curve; however, it is possible that 5HTP loading has a threshold for its effect. There is some indication of this in the studies of the effects of 5HTP on normals done by Wyatt, et al. (21) in which there was little difference between 200, 600, and 800 mg of DL-5HTP.

Tryptophan, the precursor of 5-hydroxytryptophan, could also have effects on sleep during chronic withdrawal. We have not employed tryptophan in studies to date because we have assumed that the defect produced by repeated alcohol ingestion was at the tryptophan-hydroxylase step and that the precursor most effective in correcting an abnormality of sleep would be 5-hydroxytryptophan since it is on the "other side" of the hypothesized defect.

Studies of alcoholics in the acute withdrawal stage in which fragmentation of REM sleep and decreased delta sleep is more evident also remain to be done. We would suggest that 5-hydroxytryptophan would have even more effect on the sleep of the acutely withdrawn or withdrawing alcoholic. We have not done these studies yet because we wish to test the effects of 5HTP in a group who are closer to normal using doses that are comparable to those used in normal subjects.

Another consideration in these studies is the part that nutritional disturbances play. We have chosen to neglect this (we have done so because we have a fair degree of control for these variables in that we work only with alcoholics who have not had significant liver disease or any signs of peripheral neuropathy. Our subjects are also all receiving vitamins and maintaining their weight during these studies). None of our subjects have Wernicke's syndrome or Karsakoff's psychosis. 5HTP was given during the chronic withdrawal syndrome instead of more acutely in order to control for the possibility of nutritional or vitamin deficiency disease.

Another objection to our interpretation of the data, and this well might be the most important objection, is the possibility that 5-hydroxytryptophan would act the same way in any withdrawal period following the development of tolerance and dependence to any drug. Indeed, the specificity of the effects of 5HTP following alcohol ingestion is a good subject for continuing study. We may find, for instance, that there are quantitative and not qualitative differences during withdrawal from various drugs of tolerance and dependence such as heroin, methadone, barbiturates, or amphetamines. In other words, the 5HTP effect may prove to be more related to the intensity of the sleep disruption during the development of tolerance and withdrawal and to chronic damage than it is to the type of drug used to produce the tolerance or dependence.

Another theoretic jump involves the assumption that there is an interaction between sleep regulation and daytime behavior. I suggest that at the very least, sleep regulating systems are highly correlated with other systems which regulate affect and motivation and so play some part in craving or continued drinking following tolerance development.

The process of addiction can be viewed as an acquired super-sensitivity disease. Using this model, one assumes that mixed reward and punishment systems in the brain, which are closely related to sleep regulating systems both anatomically and functionally, are abnormal in the alcoholic. The alcoholic drinks because of a need for increased stimulation of these neurons and this need is heightened during withdrawal because of denervation super-sensitivity. Using this model, we can predict that changes in sleep are going to be highly correlated with changes in this mixed punishment-reward system. Whether the two systems actually interact in a functionally significant way remains to be seen. There is some evidence that they do (22). However, we offer the hypothesis that the alcoholic begins to drink because he wishes to trigger a particular kind of activated, stimulated, mildly euphoric dream-like state. He gets some triggering of this system which is part of the brain stem mixed punishment-reward system. He continues to drink because he has to relieve the disturbance created in the systems by the administration of increasing doses of ethanol. When he finally withdraws, he suffers a denervation super-sensitivity in these systems and develops a craving for ethanol on the basis of this kind of super-sensitivity affect which is felt as subjectively uncomfortable anxiety and depression. We would also suggest that the alcoholic drinks to a point where changes in these systems are irreversible so that no matter how long he dries out, there is a continuation of the abnormalities in this system which is correlated with fragmentation of sleep and decreased delta sleep.

REFERENCES

1. Dement, W. C., Mitler, M. M., and Zarcone, V. P.: Some fundamental considerations in the study of sleep. *Psychosomatics, 24*:89-94, 1973.
2. Takahashi, Y., Kipnis, D. M., and Daughaday, W. H.: Growth hormone secretion during sleep. *J Clin Invest, 47*:2079-2090, 1968.
3. Hellman, L., Nakada, F., Curti, J., Weitzman, E. D., Kream, J., Roffwarg, H., Ellman, S., Fukushima, D. K., and Gallagher, T. F.: Cortisol is secreted episodically by normal man. *J Clin Endocrinol Metab, 30*:411-422, 1970.
4. Sassin, J., Frantz, K. G., Kapen, S., and Weitzman, E.: The nocturnal release of human prolactin in dependent on sleep. Presented at the 13th Annual Meeting of the APSS, San Diego, 1973.
5. Jouvet, M.: The role of monamines and acetylcholine containing neurons in the regulation of the sleep-waking cycle. *Rev Physiol, 64*:166-307, 1972.
6. Zarcone, V.: Marijuana and ethanol: Effects on sleep. *Psychiatry Med* (in press).
7. Greenberg, R., and Pearlman, C.: Delirium tremens and dreaming. *Am J Psychiatry, 124*:37-46, 1967.

8. Gorss, M., Goodenough, D., Tobin, M., Halpert, E., Lepore, D., Perlstein, A., et al.: Sleep disturbances and hallucinations in the acute alcoholic psychoses. *J Nerv Ment Dis, 142*:493-514, 1966.

9. Allen, R. P., Wagman, A., Faillace, L. A., and McIntosh, M.: Electroencephalographic (EEG) sleep recovery following prolonged alcohol intoxification in alcoholics. *J Nerv Ment Dis, 153*:424-433, 1971.

10. Zarcone, V., and Hoddes, E.: Effectiveness of L5-HTP on the nocturnal sleep of alcoholics. Presented at the 13th Annual Meeting of the APSS, San Diego, 1973.

11. Moir, A. T. B., and Eccleston, D.: The effects of precursor loading in the cerebral metabolism of 5-hydroxyindoles. *J Neurochem, 15*:1093-1108, 1968.

12. Aghajanian, G. K.: Influence of drugs on the firing of serotonin-containing neurons in the brain. *Fed Proc, 31*:91-96, 1972.

13. Williams, H. L., and Salamy, A.: Alcohol and sleep. In Kissin, B., and Bigleiter, H. (Ed.): *The Biology of Alcoholism: Physiology and Behavior.* New York, Pelnum Press, 1972, vol. II, pp. 435-483.

14. Pujol, J. E., Buguet, A., Froment, J. L., Jones, B., and Jouvet, M.: The central metabolism of serotonin in the cat during insomnia: a neurophysiological and biochemical study after p-chlorophenylalanine or destruction of the raphe system. *Brain Res, 29*:195-212, 1971.

15. Mouret, J. R., Froment, J. L., Bobillier, P., and Jouvet, M.: Etude neuropharmacologique et biochimique des insomnies provoquies par la p-chlorophenylalanine. *J Physiol (Paris), 59*:463-464, 1967.

16. Koella, W. P., Feldstein, A., and Czicman, J. S.: The effect of parachlorophenylalanine on the sleep of cats. *Electroencephalogr Clin Neurophysiol, 25*:481-490, 1968.

17. Jouvet, M.: Neuropharmacology of sleep. In Efrom, D. H. (Ed.): *Psychopharmacology. A Review of Progress.* Public Health Service Publication No. 1836, 1968.

18. Cohen, H., Ferguson, J., Henriksen, S., Stolk, J. M., Zarcone, V. P., Barchas, J., and Dement, W. C.: Effects of chronic depletion of brain serotonin on sleep and behavior. *Proc Am Psychol Assoc, 78*:831-832, 1970.

19. Hoyland, J., Shillito, E., Vogt, M.: The effect of parachlorophenylalanine on the behavior of cats. *Br J Pharmacol, 40*:659-667, 1970.

20. Wyatt, R. J., Engelman, K., Kupper, D. J., Sjoerdsma, A., and Snyder, F.: Effects of parachlorophenylalanine on sleep in man. *Electroencephalogr Clin Neurophysiol, 27*:529-532, 1969.

21. Wyatt, R. J., Zarcone, V. P., Engelman, K., Dement, W. C., Snyder, F., and Sjoerdsma, A.: Effects of 5-hydroxytryptophan on the sleep of normal human subjects. *Electroencephalogr Clin Neurophysiol, 30*:505-509, 1971.

22. Ellman, S. J., Ackerman, R. G., Farber, J., and Steiner, S. S.: The locus coeruleus-limbic system intracranial self-stimulation network. Presented at the 13th Annual Meeting of the APSS, San Diego, 1973.

Chapter 7

BRAIN SUBSYSTEMS IN THE GENESIS OF SCHIZOPHRENIA

Eugene Voltolina and Harvey J. Widroe

For decades scientists have hunted in vain for anatomical lesions of the brain which might be related to the genesis of schizophrenia. This frustration has led us to question our fundamental assumptions regarding our concept of schizophrenia. As a result we have come to understand schizophrenia not as a disease in itself but rather as a group of syndromes. Syndrome is here defined as a commonly occurring cluster of symptoms. Schizophrenic symptoms such as auditory hallucinations and a thought process disorder stand akin to symptoms such as cough and fever; and like the symptoms of cough and fever, hallucinations and a thought process disorder in themselves as not pathognomonic of a particular disease entity. Instead schizophrenic syndromes are the behavioral manifestations of a number of disease processes with multiple etiologies and pathogenises.

Rather than search for an ever elusive anatomical lesion, we can comprehend the pathogenises of the schizophrenic syndromes more clearly by conceptualizing the behavioral alterations observed as the product of the functional interaction within one or more of a number of brain subsystems. Our efforts at treatment then may be considered in terms of our attempts to influence this interplay of subsystems.

The etiology for a dysfunctional shift of brain subsystems leading to pathological behavior may be genetically, developmentally, and dynamically determined. For example, paranoia is an instinct characterized by fear, distrust, and hyperalertness as though one were always looking for an attacker. Under stress all men become paranoid at times, although the usual state of man is one of trust. The ability to become paranoid is genetically determined. Developmental experiences of childhood strengthen or weaken the individual's capacity for trust or distrust. Under any current dynamically significant or reality related stress an individual may or may not assume a paranoid stance. An individual demonstrates pathological paranoia when his state of distrust does not respond to mere reduction of external stress. Thus his brain mechanism for producing paranoid functioning continues to be dominant over other subsystems which in a given situation usually produce the state of trustfulness.

A cerebral subsystem which may be of great importance in our understanding of schizophrenia is the relationship between the right and left halves of the brain. In right-handed humans the left or dominant side of the brain is concerned with thought, analysis, logic, and language, while the right, or nondominant, side of the brain is concerned with feelings, intuition, and the perceptual gestalt. Electrical disturbance as evidenced in EEG abnormalities on the dominant side is likely to be associated with schizophrenia while EEG abnormalities on the nondominant side are more likely to appear associated with affective disease — especially manic depressive psychosis (1). Electrical disturbance from the nondominant or affective side of the brain can easily spread to the left side of the brain thereby producing a thought process disorder in addition to an affective disturbance. Schizo-affective or acute undifferentiated schizophrenia which are so often characterized by a thought process disorder and reality testing defect along with a pronounced affective component can be comprehended in terms of an electrical disturbance affecting both halves of the brain. In comparison, process or chronic schizophrenia with its thought process disorder and reality testing defect along with affective dullness is better understood as an electrical disturbance affecting primarily the dominant hemisphere. These concepts have certain therapeutic implications. For example, some acute schizophrenic patients do not respond at all well to phenothiazine treatment. This group of patients may have a thought process disorder and reality testing defect which are behavioral manifestations of an electrical disturbance of the nondominant cortex spreading to and overriding the dominant cortex. If this hypothesis were true, then the use of lithium, usually employed in the treatment of affective disease, plus the phenothiazine regimen should be effective in treating this otherwise treatment refractory group.

Of 126 consecutive admissions, twenty-six patients who met the criteria of acute good prognosis schizophrenia were given phenothiazines over six weeks to six months (2). Six of the twenty-six failed to respond to adequate phenothiazine treatment. All members of the group had mild nonspecific EEG abnormalities exclusively or predominantly on the nondominant side. This phenothiazine refractory group all responded to a regimen of lithium in addition to phenothiazines in anywhere from ten days to two weeks.

Another cerebral subsystem of significance in our better understanding of schizophrenia is the relationship between the limbic system and the overlying cerebral cortex. The electrical activity of the limbic system and that of the cortical system balance and regulate one another (3). Hyperactivity of one tends to produce compensatory hyperactivity in the other. Sudden cessation of activity in one releases the other. Similarly an abrupt increase in electrical activity of one may overwhelm the other.

Excessive electrical activity of the cortex may result in a grand mal seizure. The use of large quantities of phenothiazines at times has been reported to precipitate grand mal seizures. It may be that the phenothiazine action to suppress limbic system activity may release the electrical activity of the cortex resulting in a seizure. Excessive limbic system activity which overrides the cortical control may result in behavioral disturbance often clinically indistinguishable from acute schizophrenia. One might speculate in turn that acute schizophrenia is limbic system hyperactivity. It follows that phenothiazines and thioxanthines are effective in the treatment of schizophrenic psychosis by their action of decreasing limbic system hyperactivity.

Empirically, temporal lobe epilepsy is likely to respond better to a phenothiazine or thioxanthine such as halperiodol plus diphenylhydantoin than to diphenylhydantoin and/or phenobarbital alone (4, 5). This fact strongly suggests that temporal lobe epilepsy is often a subcortical or limbic system hyperactivity which overwhelms the damaged temporal cortex. This hypothesis also explains the phenomenon of some patients who after starting diphenylhydantoin develop hallucinations, delusions, and depersonalization. In these patients the diphenylhydantoin decreases the ability of the temporal cortex to withstand the electrical excitation of the underlying limbic system. Patients whose temporal lobe epilepsy seems to worsen when given diphenylhydantoin deserve treatment with haloperidol, trifluperazine, or some other limbic system suppressant.

CONCLUSION

The pathogenesis of schizophrenia may be clarified by elaboration of the brain subsystem concept. Further elaboration of this concept may enable us as clinicians to develop and test new hypotheses concerning treatment.

REFERENCES

1. Flor-Henry, P.: Schizophrenic-like reaction and affective psychoses associated with temporal lobe epilepsy: Etiological factors. *Am J Psychiatry, 126*:400, 1961.
2. Voltolina, E.: A defined subgroup of treatment refractory good prognosis schizophrenics. *Biol Psychiatry* (in press).
3. Smythies, J.: *Brain Mechanisms and Behavior.* New York, Acad Pr, 1970.
4. Detre, T., and Feldman, F.: Behavior disorder associated with seizure states: Pharmacological and psychosocial management. In Glaser, G. (Ed.): *EEG and Behavior.* New York, Basic, 1962.
5. Pavig, P., Deluca, M., and Osterheld, R.: Thioridazine hydrochloride in the treatment of behavioral disorders in epileptics. *Am J Psychiatry, 1179*:832, 1961.

Chapter 8

INCREASING CEREBRAL FUNCTION IN BRAIN-DAMAGED PATIENTS

HARVEY J. WIDROE

PSYCHIATRISTS are frequently called upon to distinguish whether the etiology of a given patient's problem is "functional" or "organic" in nature. While this distinction is often far from clear, it nonetheless has significant implications for treatment. Ten years ago the determination of an organic etiology meant one could do little to help a patient; on the other hand, the determination of a functional etiology often suggested a distinctly better prognosis. At the same time in some instances patients with organic brain damage after treatment demonstrated a substantial improvement in overall cerebral functioning. Thus the impressive results of gait or speech training after a cerebral vascular accident prove that patients with significant impairment of functioning secondary to organic brain damage can be successfully treated. Modalities of treatment other than training programs may likewise yield positive results. For example, patients with psychoses secondary to tertiary lues after metrazol convulsive treatment may remit to a nonpsychotic state (1). Of greater significance is our increasing knowledge of the beneficial effects that psychoactive drugs can have on cerebral functioning.

In our earlier efforts to increase cerebral functioning by psychopharmacological intervention, we used a trial and error approach based on a few unfounded assumptions and clinical intuition modified by day-to-day experience. Our major operational assumption in efforts to improve cerebral functioning was that one neuron can be taught or conditioned to do the work that two neurons had done previously. While contributing to a pleasant set of images, this assumption had little relation to what we have come to learn about brain function.

Current attempts to increase the level of functioning of damaged brains are based on four principles more closely related to empirical data.

1. Sick neurons can improve. Psychiatrists tend to forget what every neurosurgeon depends upon, that a nonfunctioning neuron may be sick rather than dead. Any agent which decreases edema, increases oxygen or blood supply, or aids in improving cellular nutrition may enable a given sick neuron to return to some semblance of normal functioning.

2. Neurons can develop new axonal or dendritic connections either as a function of development or regeneration after trauma. Neurons which produce monoamines as neurotransmitters have a significant capacity for exhibiting growth plasticity in the adult brain and spinal cord. Cut axons have been found to sprout vigorously new axons that enter and supply nerves to structures in the brain not previously innervated by this group of axons. In areas where innervation has been removed, the monoamine producing axons appear to sprout and re-innervate the vacated synaptic sites. A related observation is that nerve cells near damaged cells move in to fill the vacancy. This filling in process may be interpreted as a form of reorganization. Major therapeutic implications lie in the question of which experiential events and which other conditions enhance the proliferation of dendritic connections or axonal regeneration so as to produce "re-wiring" of functional systems. It is possible that training programs for brain-damaged patients may be effective as a result of this mechanism.

3. (a) Events at synapses can be influenced, and (b) the efficiency of axonal conduction can be increased.

   This principle has been demonstrated in the vast body of data concerning the modes of action of psychoactive drugs. For example, amphetamines, tricyclic antidepressants, and monamine oxidase inhibitors all have significant effects upon the release and reuptake of norepinephrine. In addition, lithium affects the stability of postsynaptic membranes, while diphenylhydantoin increases the efficiency of axonal conduction.

Apart from the multiple neurochemical means of effecting the action of neurotransmitters, certain experiences of the organism also affect synaptic events. Thus, the natural stress of fighting leads to (a) lowered affinity for reuptake of norepinephrine into nerve endings of the cerebral cortex, (b) an increase in the number of uptake sites, and (c) lowered affinity for dextroamphetamine (2).

4. Certain areas of the brain can be affected by psychoactive agents more readily than other areas. These areas exist in a balance of subsystems, each regulating the electrical outflow of several others. When this functional equilibrium is disturbed, many kinds of psychopathology result. Psychopharmacological agents affect this equilibrium, and as a consequence both normal and psychopathological behavior will be profoundly influenced.

The balance of brain subsystems is well illustrated by arousal behavior. Wakefulness is related to stimulation of the neocortex by impulses from the reticular activating system (3). If the reticular activating system does not fire its arousal pattern, the animal sleeps, and the cortex shows sleep patterns of electrical behavior. On the other hand, the cortex may receive a stimulus, code it, classify it, compare it, and interpret its consequences.

It may subsequently "tell" the reticular activating system that no real danger is present and that no alerting is necessary, or it may trigger an alerting response.

Chlorpromazine dampens the electrical activity of the reticular activating system. If we ascribe a highly agitated hyperalert state to cortical overflow secondary to hyperactivity of the reticular activating system, then diminution of reticular activating system activity by the use of chlorpromazine will decrease hyperalertness and agitated behavior.

Another example of a psychopharmacological agent affecting brain subsystems in a differential manner is the affect of haloperidol on the amygdaloid nucleus. If the temporal cortex and amygdaloid nucleus exist in a functional balance with cortical activity usually supressing activity of the amygdaloid nucleus, then in some patients cortical acting sedatives will release the amygdaloid activity with cortical spiking and violent behavior as a result. Similarly, in patients who are prone to violent outbursts with concomitant temporal lobe abnormalities of the cortex demonstrable on EEG, haloperidol by suppressing amygdaloid spiking may suppress aggression. This often occurs in the very patient whose behavioral symptoms were more pronounced after use of a cortical acting sedative such as diazepam or even diphenylhydantoin. The haloperidol suppression of the amygdaloid is noted, especially if the lesion is on the nondominant side, the side which seems to be more concerned with affective disturbance.

These four principles have enabled us to make more sensible judgments about which medications may increase a given patient's level of cerebral functioning. We classify current choices of psychoactive agents according to the specific type of brain damage present.

Hyperkinetic Adolescents

While the concept of hyperkinetic child includes a great many subgroups, the positive effects of methylphenidate and the amphetamines are thought to be secondary to an increase in attention span with a subsequent decrease in distractability and agitation (4). For the hyperkinetic adolescent chlorpromazine in addition to methylpenidate helps check impulse flooding of the cortex via the limbic system. In some instances inclusion of diphenylhydantoin in the psychopharmacological regimen may produce dramatic effects.

Cerebral Vascular Accidents

Cerebral vasodilators can greatly increase cerebral functioning at motor, affective, and intellective levels. Papaverine and ergot alkaloids, cerebral vasodilators acting in two different modes, may conjointly increase the blood supply to sick neurons adjacent to an infarcted area to the extent that they receive nutrition sufficient for a return to functioning.

Dextroamphetamine by increasing attention span and aiding

in the organization of thought processes may also be useful in patients whose intellectual functions are impaired post-CVA.

Trifluoperazine as a representative of the nonsedating phenothiazines seems to decrease agitation by limbic system suppression. If a patient's agitation continues, a moderately sedating phenothiazine such as prochlorperazine or perphenazine may be more effective. In some patients with great agitation the maximally sedating phenothiazines such as thioridazine or chlorpromazine may be required; however, the clinician must be aware that maximally sedating phenothiazines may intensify or produce an acute brain syndrome and thereby increase intellective impairment.

Diphenylhydantoin should always be employed in a patient's CVA therapeutic regimen in order to increase the efficiency of neural conductivity.

If the patient is profoundly depressed and amphetamines only produce a transient improvement in his affective state, then a monoamine oxidase inhibitor such as isocarboxazid or a nonsedating tricyclic such as imipramine may be employed. Monoamine oxidase inhibitors are to be preferred because of the decreased likelihood of producing an acute brain syndrome such as that produced by a combination of the antidepressant and other psychoactive medications. Tricyclic antidepressants combined with other psychoactive agents commonly produce a recent memory defect, poor judgment, and confusion.

Amphetamine Addiction

Brain damage secondary to amphetamine addiction usually consists of widespread multiple miniscule cerebral cortical infarcts secondary to acute vasospasm of cortical arterioles directly after amphetamine usage, especially by an intravenous route of administration.

Nonsedating phenothiazines control the paranoia commonly encountered and aid in reducing the torrent of grossly scattered thinking. Former amphetamine addicts demonstrate symptoms of cortical impairment months after they have desisted from amphetamine abuse. The acute withdrawal from amphetamines is no more severe than forty-eight to seventy-two hours of sleepiness, depression, hyperirritability and lethargy. But it may take months for the amphetamine addict to become capable of thinking coherently and feeling interest in anything or anyone except that which smacks of bizarre narcissistic borderline thinking.

Heroin Addiction

While methadone withdrawal and maintenance is the currently fashionable practice, in reality an increasing number of psychiatrists are greatly disillusioned with methadone as a treatment tool. During acute withdrawal the methadone treated heroin addict is rarely comfortable. In addition he presents an endless series of demands and complaints to doctors and nursing staff. Many methadone treated heroin addicts sign out against medical advice in order to obtain more heroin. Those who stay in the hospital are reknowned for behavior massively disruptive to the ward milieu. Because of these problems, plus the high recidivist rate among heroin addicts who have completed acute detoxification with methadone, some hospitals are altogether giving up acute detoxification programs for heroin addicts.

A more effective technique for withdrawing and treating the heroin addict is based in part on our neurophysiological understanding of where and how heroin affects brain function. Heroin acts by poisoning the pleasure centers located along the median forebrain bundle to the extent that only heroin administration can set off the experience of pleasure. Thus we can comprehend why heroin addicts relinquish the usual modalities of obtaining pleasure — such as sex, food, and work — and shift to a world based on taking drugs or recalling the drug experience (observed as obsessive talk about drug experiences). Since the pleasure centers in the median forebrain bundle respond to little else except heroin, the addict readily relinquishes his usual, but currently ineffectual, modalities of obtaining pleasure. Even after a single heroin experience these centers are affected for weeks. Jones reports absence of morning penile erection and the absence of sexual dreams for weeks after a single heroin exposure (see Ch. 5). In patients who have been addicted less than two years, functional recovery of these centers is possible after six or more drug-free months. Patients who have been addicted more than two years may have substantial permanent damage to the median forebrain bundle pleasure centers.

Acute heroin withdrawal can be achieved most comfortably for the patient and most tolerably for those in the patient's environment by the administration of massive doses of maximally sedating phenothiazines (thioridazine or chlorpramazine) along with large amounts of chlordiazepoxide. Thioridazine is to be preferred to chlorpromazine because it has less of a hypotensive effect. The hyperactivity of both cortical and limbic systems secondary to heroin withdrawal is diminished by administration of these two agents, the chlordiazepoxide acting at the cortical level, while the phenothiazine acts at the limbic system level. Patients under treatment with this regimen are relatively comfortable, are less likely to flee the treatment environment, and as a rule are not disruptive to the ward milieu.

After the acute withdrawal period of seven to fourteen days, the dosages of medication can be lowered 50 per cent: it is imperative that they not be discontinued. At this point patients frequently report that the cravings which commonly return the addict to heroin after acute withdrawal are diminished in intensity. It is advisable to continue this regimen for a number of months until the patient shows substantial improvement in his level of intellectual and social functioning and the absence of cravings. These events are often clinically concomitant with the onset of a period of depression.

LSD

The acute brain syndrome secondary to LSD is best treated with moderately or maximally sedating phenothiazines. While the clinical site of chronic LSD damage is not clear, evidence for LSD related organic brain damage continues to mount. Organic damage shows up on psychological test results, clinical observation, and in the presence of cerebrospinal fluid CPK. In the treatment of the chronic phase symptoms, flashbacks can be eliminated by prochlorperazine, diazepam, or a combination of the two. Since diazepam is more effective, we can presume that its anticonvulsant properties decrease the low threshold firing of rods and cones and other neurons in the visual system. The intellective and affective deficits secondary to chronic LSD abuse over a period of months may respond to a regimen of amphetamines plus nonsedating or moderately sedating phenothiazines.

Parkinsonism

Patients with Parkinsonism demonstrate a high incidence of depression. Only recently have we come to understand that this depressive state is more than a psychological reaction to the disability and incapacity produced by Parkinsonism. The Parkinsonism symptoms and the depression are both related to monoamine deficits, especially a lack of dopamine in the extra pyramidyl system. L-dopa, which is metabolized to dopamine in the brain, produces symptomatic improvement in Parkinsonian symptoms and a general improvement in the depressive state. Of course, the clinician must be concerned that excess dopamine in the limbic system will lead to cortical overflow of impulses with a subsequent acute brain syndrome or an affective psychosis.

Idiopathic Temporal Lobe Damage

Idiopathic temporal lobe damage as manifest by psychosis, dyscontrol syndrome, or borderline character behavior may be ascertained by EEG, especially with nasopharangeal leads. It responds surprisingly well to diphenylhydantoin, mephobarbital, diazepam, or primidone. If the use of the anticonvulsants makes the behavioral manifestations more pronounced, then the patient may be suffering from temporal lobe dysfunction as a result of amygdaloid nucleus overflow. In such instances fluphenazine, trifluoperazine, or haloperidol should be used instead of the usual anticonvulsants (5).

Alcohol or Barbiturate Related
Degenerative Brain Damage

The withdrawal of any cortical acting sedative to which tolerance has been acquired, whether it be alcohol, barbiturates, meprobamate, or diazepam, results in severe withdrawal symptoms with generalized hyperactivity of the nervous system. In every instance save one (ethchlorvinol) a shift to another cortical acting sedative which is gradually reduced over a period of time seems to be the basic principle for managing the withdrawal in a safe and relatively comfortable fashion. Ethchlorvinol dosage must be reduced gradually while the patient is in a structured setting. Vitamin deficiency may contribute to the acute brain syndrome of withdrawal and produce Korsakoff's psychosis.

The chronic brain damage resulting from cortical acting sedative usually includes frontal lobe damage manifest as poor judgment as well as defect of fine nuance of affect. Affective volatility secondary to poor cortical control over the limbic system is also prominent. Improved cortical functioning can result from treatment with amphetamines, nonsedating phenothiazines (to reduce limbic system override of the damaged cortex) and diphenylhydantoin which effectively increases the efficiency of neuronal firing.

While these schemata for treating patients with damaged brains have produced noteworthy results to date, we look eagerly to the basic brain function research of the next decade to suggest techniques which will augment our ability to constructively alter cerebral functioning.

REFERENCES

1. Rapaport, D., Kenyon, V., and Lazoff, M.: Note on Metrazol in General Paresis. *Psychiatry, 4*:165-176, 1941.
2. Henley, E., Moisset, M., and Welch, B.: Catecholamine uptake in cerebral cortex: Adaptive change induced by fighting. *Science, 180*:1050-1052, 1973.
3. Smythies, J.: *Brain Mechanism and Behavior.* New York, Acad Pr, 1970, pp.

113-115.
4. Wender, P.: Some speculations concerning a possible biochemical basis of minimal brain dysfunction. In de la Cruz, et al. (Eds.): *Minimal Brain Dysfunction.* New York, NY Acad Sci, 1973, pp. 18-28.
5. Detre, T., and Feldman, F.: Behavior disorder associated with seizure states: Pharmacological and psychosocial management. In Glaser, G. (Ed.): *EEG and Behavior.* New York, Basic, 1962.

AUTHOR INDEX

A

Achenbach, K., 23
Ackerman, R. G., 92
Adkins, R. J., 64
Adler, C., 23
Aghajanian, G. K., 92
Ajuriaguerra, J., 22
Allen, R. P., 92
Allen, 83
Amassian, V. E., 63

B

Bach-y-Rita, George, v, 24, 34, 35
Bailey, P., 63
Barchas, J., 92
Bard, P., 28, 34
Barrett, B., 19, 23
Benton, A. L., 21
Betz, 58
Biedenbach, M. A., 64
Bigleiter, H., 92
Blake, William, 38
Bobillier, P., 92
Bogen, J. E., 4, 20, 21, 23
Bonsignoria, A., 34
Brodel, 61
Brodman, K., 63
Brooks, L. R., 18, 23
Broverman, D. M., 22
Bruner, J., 23
Bryn, G. W., 21
Buchsbaum, M., 10, 22
Bucy, P. C., 28, 34
Budzynski, T. H., 23
Buguet, A., 92
Burke, R. E., 64
Butler, S. R., 22

C

Cajal, S., 63
Callaway, Enoch, v, 65, 76
Campbell, A. M. G., 57
Campbell, 40
Campbell, A. W., 63
Cassaway, E., 76
Chang, H. T., 64
Climent, C. E., 35
Cohen, R. A., 20, 23, 92
Conners, C. K., 20, 23
Corkin, S., 21
Critchley, M., 9, 22
Curti, J., 91
Czicman, J. S., 92

D

Dalton, K., 34
Daughaday, W. H., 91
Dax, 4
Day, R. S., 22
Delgado, J. M. R., 28, 29, 30, 34
Deluca, M., 96
Dement, W. C., 91, 92
DenHyer, K., 19, 23
DeQuincy, Thomas, 53, 57
Detre, T., 96, 100
DeZure, R., 23
Doyle, J. C., 11, 22
Drachman, David A., 57

E

Eccles, J. C., 64
Eccleston, D., 92
Economo, C, von, 63
Efrom, D. H., 92

107

SUBJECT INDEX

A

Abnormal serotonergic mechanisms of sleep regulation in alcoholism, 77-92
Acetylcholine, 80
Acute heroin withdrawal, 103
Acute schizophrenia, 95
Acute undifferentiated schizophrenia, 94
Acute withdrawal from amphetamines, 102
Addiction, heroin, 102, 103
Addiction to alcohol, symptoms in withdrawal, 44
Aggression,
  brain stimulation and, 29
  neurophysiological mechanisms of, 27-30
Aggressive patients, clinical aspects of, 30-34
Aggressive behavior
  biological basis of, clinical aspects, 24-35
  effects of gonadal steroids on, 27
Agijanian, 88
Alcohol, 38, 39, 41, 43, 44, 49
Alcohol or barbiturate related degenerative brain damage, 105
Alcoholics, 39, 43
Alcoholic withdrawal syndrome, chronic, 78
Alcoholics Anonymous, 55
Alcoholism, 77
  sleep regulation in, abnormal serotonergic mechanisms of, 77-92
Alpha feedback training, 20
Alpha predominance,
  parietal, 16
  temporal, 16
Alpha ratios,
  average, 11
  differences, 16
Ambidexterity and lateralization in left-handed people, 17-19
Amnesia, 33

Amphetamines, 38, 45, 48, 65, 69, 70, 71, 82, 90, 98, 100
  acute withdrawal from, 102
  addiction, 101, 102
  clinical response to, 69
Amygdala,
  bilateral removal of, 28
  stimulation of, 29
  suppression of, 100
Amygdaloid nucleus, 99
Analytic functions, 3
Anoxia, 42
Anterior motor horn cells, 62
Anticonvulsants, 104
Antidepressants, 82, 98
"Antisocial personality," 26
Aphasia, permanent, 21
Aphrodisiacs, 41, 45
Arteriograms, 33
Assaultive patients, 24
Asymmetry,
  EEG, biofeedback training for voluntary control of, 19, 20
  task-dependent, 16
Attention-to-breath task, 16
Auditory hallucinations, 93
Autonomic nervous system, 44
  long-persisting disturbances in the, 44
Averaged evoked potentials (AEP), 67

B

Barbiturate or alcohol related degenerative brain damage, 105
Barbiturates, 44, 48, 49, 82, 90
Betz cells, 59
Beyond the Pleasure Principle, 37
Bilateral language representation, 18
Binomial Tests, 85
Biofeedback training for voluntary control of EEG asymmetry, 19, 20

111